ADAM

A Story of Life and Death . . . and Love

Stephen MacKenzie

ADAM

A Story of Life and Death...and Love

ISBN 13: 978-0-9979317-5-4
Library of Congress PCN: 2017946916

Inquiries should be addressed to:
www.amitypublications.com

To contact the author, please visit
stephen-mackenzie.com

Printed in the United States of America

Dedication

This book is dedicated to the family of Adam Routhier, especially his mother, sister, and grandmother with whom I have grown so close over the years. This work would not have been possible had they not been willing to shed their tears, share their love, and bare their souls as they brought me into and through the brightest and darkest places, and the most hopeful and hopeless points in their lives.

And to Adam's friends, who shared their memories and their stories in the most open and honest ways. I could not have survived those early days and weeks had it not been for your love and support, and I certainly could not have written this book.

I love you all so much and I am forever in your debt. You have blessed and enriched my live in unimaginable ways.

Table of Contents

A Note from the Author

This is a work of nonfiction. With very few exceptions, only for purposes of clarity, every word uttered, every laugh emitted, every tear shed is as true an account of what actually happened in Adam's life as I could manage to tell. However, in order to protect their privacy I have changed most of the names of those who contributed material for this book. The only real names I have used are mine, Sandy Crockett's and, with his mom's permission, Adam's.

Stephen MacKenzie

Acknowledgement

There are several other people whose help has been critical to this book making it from emotional desire to published reality:

My stepdaughter Donna Berube, one of only two proofreaders of the earliest drafts;

My friend and former pastor, Anne Robertson, for her advice, feedback and support;

My friend and English 401 instructor Tamara Neidzolkowski, without whom I would never have become an English teacher;

My wife MaryAnne MacKenzie, who not only read my earliest drafts but supported me during the long hours and emotional process of writing this book;

And finally my friend and publisher Layne Case and copyeditor Nancy Grossman, whose enthusiastic support and encouragement actually made me believe.

Introduction

Death ends a life, not a relationship.
– Morrie Schwartz

The catalyst for this book was a tragic event that happened the night of September 10, 2004, an event I found out about when I picked up the newspaper from my driveway on the morning of the 11th. I shall never forget that Saturday morning, nor the headline that quickly caught my eye: *Man killed in crash: 18-year-old loses control of vehicle in Somersworth.* Somersworth . . . Oh God, I must know him . . . And then the next line . . . *An 18-year-old local man was killed in a single-car accident on Indigo Hill Road.* And then the next . . . *Adam Routhier was pronounced dead at the crash scene by Somersworth emergency personnel*. Oh, my God . . . Adam. I walked back into the house and just about collapsed into my wife's arms.

Adam Routhier's entrance into my life helped begin one of the brightest periods of my entire teaching career, and his exit one of the darkest. We had been so close for most of his four years at Somersworth High—maybe too close, maybe not close enough. Our relationship was professional. I was his teacher. But it was also personal. I was his friend. Not his buddy, but his friend.

When I was a kid, I spent a week each July or August at my church's summer camp, Wanakee. Every site had 16 to 20 boys and girls with two adult counselors, one a paid intern and one a volunteer. Of all my terrific childhood memories of Wanakee, one thing never faded and it eventually made it into my classroom. Even as a little boy, I can remember thinking during those weeks at camp, *Wow! I feel like the most important person in the world to my counselors*. I know I wasn't exactly, at least I was no more important than any of the other kids, but I wasn't any less important either. That's how they made me feel. And that's how

I've always wanted my students to feel, every single one of them, like when we're together, they're the most important people in the world to me . . . *because they are.*

Where my way of thinking became problematic was with the occasional pushback I got from colleagues and the Teachers' Association. *Don't get too close to your students. Don't get too personal with your students. Avoid physical contact with your students. Never hug your students.* Yet, I high-five, fist-bump, and hug my students all the time. What do I do when students come up to me with their arms outstretched—shove an arm out to shake their hand? Or even worse, should I actually say to them, as I once heard a colleague do, *Nope, I won't hug you but I'll shake your hand*? Seriously? I can't do it. How important would that kid feel he or she was to me?

My last words to Adam were, "I love you, Adam." His last words to me were, "I love you too, Mr. Mac." We were on the football field and his graduation ceremony had just concluded. We never saw each other again. Our paths just didn't happen to cross that summer and then he was dead. He was not my little brother or my son. He was not a nephew or a cousin. He was just my student, but he was definitely part of my family and I was part of his.

Within weeks of Adam's death I was sure I wanted to write about him but it has taken years to figure out why. I knew I wanted his family and closest friends to contribute. In fact, in a way they did more of the writing than I did. Many people sat for several hours and put their memories into a Word document, often working hard, so I was told, to keep the keyboards dry. This book is, in essence, a compilation and structuring of those memories. The result is my attempt to share it all with you, to show you a life that ended way too early yet touched so many, to maybe, in a way, bring *you* into Adam's close circle of friends. And while the book is nonfiction, its pages contain all the humor of a comedy, the horror of a tragedy, the language and emotion of a drama, and the passion of a love story—ours and his.

Adam's death was *the* defining moment of my career in education. It resulted in weeks of tears, many hours of emotional anguish, and weekly lunches for months with his—our—group of friends. These were actually more group therapy sessions than social get-togethers, and they began tight friendships that normally would never have lasted this long.

It's been more than ten years, but in a few days I am heading to a Red Sox game with one of our mutual friends. Next month several of us will take Adam's mother out to dinner on his birthday—as always. And on Christmas Eve afternoon, we will gather at her apartment. I'll bring my still-warm apple pie, she'll have the coffee on, and we will hug, talk, celebrate, and love. We have not missed a Christmas Eve afternoon together since December 24, 2004. Charlene once said, "I look forward to this so much. It's the highlight of my Christmas." I have no doubt she meant it. It's a highlight of ours as well.

I should probably tell you, too, that part of my wanting to write this book was because I knew that somewhere there lived, assuming he was still alive, a man who might as well have been signed up as a sperm donor. A man I don't know, have never met, who never paid a dime of child support, and who never had the brains nor the balls to be a part of Adam's life. That might be a good reason to want to embarrass, even humiliate someone, but it wasn't a good enough reason to write a book. There was more than that, and I finally figured it out.

The thing is, Adam was everything I was not, and yet he loved me anyway. I required work of him he didn't want to do. I asked him to "go places" he didn't want to go. I asked him to consider ideas and issues he didn't want to think about. Yet, when things got dark for him, when life pressures increased too much and daily living got almost unbearable, it was me he turned to for help, in large part because he knew he was one of mine, one of the most important people in the world to me. Maybe part of me is looking for forgiveness, for not being able to keep him alive. But a bigger part of me wants him to somehow know that even after all these years, he's still one of the most important people in the world to me.

Book One

Mr. Mac and Family

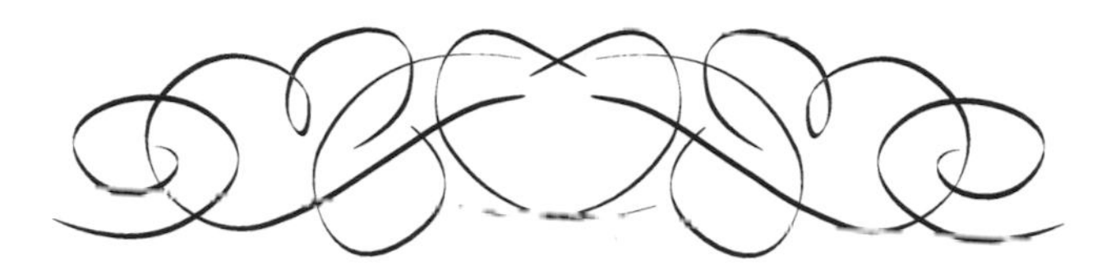

Chapter 1: Mr. Mac

I first met Adam in the fall of 2000, the beginning of his freshman year at Somersworth High School. I had been teaching English at Somersworth High for four years at the time, and though I did happen to have a section of Freshman English that fall Adam was not in it. It was in the weight room after school where I ran into him and his group of friends (though they have always maintained that we actually met by the cash register in Cumberland Farms the summer before). Although I did not lift what they did, nor bench what they did, nor max what they did I think they had some respect for the fact that a forty-three-year-old guy who weighed about a hundred and thirty pounds and had a thirty inch waist was pressing thirty-five pound free weights, twenty-pound flies, and twenty-five pound concentration curls—three sets of eight reps each. And on alternate days I would do a hundred crunches and another hundred push-ups. Anyway, that was how we met, with me being slightly jealous of him and his friends (and their abilities on both the football field and a workout bench) and them being tolerant of me . . . and patient.

Eventually we became something close to friends. In the weight room, I could be just another guy—sort of—and it'd be two more years before I'd have any of them in class. They helped me with my routines and spotted me when necessary. I did the same for them. Their help was typically along the lines of "no bending those elbows," and "come on, come on—push, up, more, harder, you can do this!" My help was more like, "wow!" A respectful camaraderie was born nonetheless and we all really began to like each other.

I remember one day when about five of us were working out together. There came a few minutes when we all happened to be between sets and a conversation started. They had some questions about me and my class. I did my best to answer them.

. . . Yes, I've lived in Somersworth since 1989.
. . . No, I was born in Dover and grew up in Rollinsford.
. . . Yup, the farthest away I've ever lived—if you don't count the three months a year I used to live in the Dominican Republic--was when I was first married and we lived on Northwood Lake in Epsom.
. . . Yes, I've been married since 1978.
. . . Yes, to the same woman.
. . . Yes, my senior honor students write five-to-seven-page essays and eight-to-ten-page research papers with eight to ten outside sources, using proper MLA formatting and documentation.
. . . Maybe not now, but you will be able to write those essays if I'm lucky enough to have you in Honors English IV—and, by the way, that would be "my friends and I."

Eventually they started talking about some of their classes and teachers, what they were good at, who they liked (and didn't), and I did have to say, more than once, "Guys, you can't trash-talk my colleagues to me." They talked about how badly they had treated one of their math teachers, and that they actually felt bad about it. They talked about the football team, their coaches, and practices. They talked about their *unofficial* initiation onto the team that included making their way through the infamous "swamp" and running the gauntlet of spanking girls. Adam told about how well he pretended to hate it. They also talked about how much they hated French class and how much their French teacher, Monsieur Bleau, hated them. I said I doubted that was true and then continued with, "Come on, you guys, cut the man some slack. Can you imagine what it'd be like to be a kid growing up in America with the last name Bleau?" I watched their eyes drop into glazed thinking for several moments before Kenneth Head slowly nodded and said, "Yup."

Adam started laughing first, and then the others erupted. I had no idea then how far it would take us, but my journey with Adam Routhier and that group of kids had begun. For others, though, their journey with Adam had begun years before . . .

Chapter 2: Charlene

Despite being divorced from her daughter's father and single at the time, Charlene was happy when she found out she was pregnant with Adam. There were seven years between Jenny and Adam but she felt the same happiness with both of them. Of course there was the discomfort, also some guilt, about being an unwed mother, to say nothing about also being divorced. So she was embarrassed to tell her parents about the pregnancy. Theirs was a Roman Catholic home and people waited until they were married to live together and have sex, but . . . well . . . anyway, she was happy, and she thinks her folks were happy for her. At least they were happy to welcome another grandchild into the family, likely in part because Charlene had taken back her maiden name, which meant another generation of Routhiers to carry on.

A mother's bias notwithstanding, Charlene will tell you Adam was a beautiful baby, beautiful and so happy. According to her, everyone loved him, especially his sister, Jenny. Adam was her "baby brover." At the time he was born they lived in the Bartlett Avenue housing project in a two-bedroom apartment. A few months later they moved into a three-bedroom apartment in the same complex, and while Charlene continued working as a nursing assistant she started attending a job-training class at Somersworth High School. All things considered she was pretty happy.

Evidently Adam's father was pretty happy too, but for different reasons. He didn't have a car or a place to live. He was the kind of guy who couldn't hold a job for very long and could always find someone else to blame when he got fired or quit. Mostly, so it would seem, he was happy to settle down for a bit and have someone take care of him. It didn't take Charlene long to figure out he was never going to be a good husband nor a responsible father.

Consequently, with two children and a freeloader to support,

Charlene figured she really needed to change careers and registered in an adult ed program. As part of her job training she did some clerical work at Pease Air Force Base in Newington, NH. At about the same time, Portsmouth Naval Shipyard was looking for an office person to work in one of the recruiting departments. Charlene was able to land the job and still works there today. The new job not only paid more money but provided her and her children with excellent health insurance. In addition, because she was a single working mother with two children, she qualified for subsidized housing where the rent was based on her income—and her income was all she had.

Joe—that's Adam's father—wasn't even with them a year before it became clear that not only was he an irresponsible guy, he was actually a dangerous guy. Charlene finally told him he had to move out, but he would not go quietly. He kept coming back, bothering the children, pestering Charlene, and disrupting the household. He was just not going to willingly accept Charlene's wishes and leave. On two different occasions he went on a rampage in the apartment and wrecked a lot of her things. Eventually he did clear out, but only because he'd ended up in jail—for breaking and entering. Go figure. What they ultimately discovered was that he had habits to support, so the burglaries were not really a surprise. Charlene was just glad to finally be rid of him.

After Joe spent several months in jail, Charlene received a letter from him saying he wanted her to bring Adam to visit him. He said if she didn't he was going to get a lawyer and make her bring him. Shortly thereafter she received another letter from a guardian ad litem telling her she had to speak with him regarding Joe. Charlene met with the guardian and was warned that she had to let Joe visit with Adam whether she wanted him to or not—he was Adam's father and he had rights. Charlene was scared. She didn't want Joe in Adam's life for fear of their safely, but she clearly had no choice.

> *What happened was, the guardian made an appointment for a visitation. Since Joe was out of jail by that time, the visit was going to be at the guardian's office. I brought Adam but only because I was afraid I would get into trouble if I didn't. Well, Joe never showed*

up. The guardian made a second appointment and Joe didn't show up for that one either. I was so glad. The guardian found out what kind of person Joe was. Before too long Joe relinquished all rights to Adam and never bothered me again. I would still get scared every once in a while that he'd show up at my door, but thank God he never did. The only good thing that came out of that awful relationship was Adam.

* * *

A little over a year after Charlene finally got Joe out of her life, she was fixed up with a guy named Warren. She didn't really want to talk about him but he was part of Adam's life for a while. She thought at the time that he was the right one, for her and for her children. He was a divorced father with two sons. The boys lived with their mother but Warren had regular visitation. One of them was about two years older than Adam. The other was the same age as Jenny. Adam got along pretty well with both of them.

Once Charlene and Warren started dating things progressed quickly. She moved out of her Bartlett Avenue apartment—a bad decision in hindsight—and they moved into an apartment together in Rochester, probably another bad decision. Charlene went to work each day and Adam went to a babysitter. Before long they bought a trailer in Rochester and got married. It had been a fairly rocky engagement. He'd get mad and then she'd get mad. They even called off the wedding at one point. Eventually, though, they went through with the ceremony at Charlene's sister's house in Exeter. The marriage lasted all of about two years.

The problem with Warren was that he didn't want to share anything. He didn't want to be a couple but more like married singles, roommates kind of, or I guess kids today would say, "friends with benefits." To him, my kids were mine and his kids were his. They played with each other a lot when they were together, but Warren never really got close to either Jenny or Adam. He also made it hard on me financially because I was paying for childcare along with all the other bills. We would split the bills in half, but I didn't have much say in what bills we ran up. I remember one time he went to the store—I didn't even know he was going—and bought all kinds of stuff for the yard: push brooms, shovels, rakes, I don't know what all. He gave me the bill and told me what I owed him. He just did things like that. I was broke almost all the time.

A few months after they were married, Warren received some money when the house he'd owned with his ex-wife was sold. He bought some land in South Berwick and moved their trailer onto it. He didn't include Charlene in any of the decision making, and bought the land in just his name. Before long the marriage went downhill. He wasn't her husband, he was her landlord.

Adam was almost five when Charlene and Warren divorced, and all of a sudden she was scrambling for a place to live. The trailer was actually in both names but, because it was on his land, Warren ended up with everything. Charlene couldn't afford a lawyer, couldn't afford to move the trailer even if she could have gotten it, and just wasn't very good at fighting. She ended up broke as usual, but by that time everything was done. They were all glad to be rid of him, especially Charlene.

* * *

After her divorce from Warren, Charlene and the kids moved in with her parents for a while. Adam went to Somersworth Daycare back on Bartlett Avenue, and graduated from pre-school there. Eventually they found an apartment in South Berwick, Maine because that's where Jenny was going to school. Charlene was able to find another child care provider for Adam and would drop him off on her way to work. When he started first grade he was able to attend school with the other kids he knew from daycare.

For a while, things were fairly decent for the Routhiers. But Charlene still had money problems—being a single working mom of two young children was definitely not easy financially. It wasn't emotionally easy, either. During these difficult years Charlene, developed a coping strategy: drinking. The drinking became a serious problem, something she was not proud of and did not admit easily. Still, she managed to hold down a responsible job, maintain a home for her family, and keep them all fed.

> *Adam went to Central School in South Berwick. I do have to say he was never an angel in grade school. His teacher said he was a troublemaker. She told me he talked and fooled around in class all the time. I remember Adam telling me that the teacher didn't like him and that some of the other kids would call him "A-dumb." I probably should have been more involved in his education but it seemed like I always had to work, and missing work meant missing money which I couldn't afford to miss. I tried but maybe I could have tried harder.*

While living in South Berwick, Adam joined the Cub Scouts, which according to Charlene, he really liked. She smiles at the memories of how cute he looked in his little uniform with its neckerchief and all. He loved playing with the other kids at the meetings. And he *really* loved the camp outs they sometimes had.

Adam also developed a strong passion for video games, particularly Mario Brothers. One day Charlene needed to do some shopping at Walmart. While she shopped Adam planted himself in front of one of the video games they had out for the kids to play—I mean what better way to con a mom into buying a game than to let her kids play it for free, right? The problem was Charlene had no intentions of buying it, but when she was done shopping Adam wasn't done playing. She couldn't get him to leave. He was so involved with the game that he stood there playing until he peed his pants. Finally she took his hands off the joy sticks, which by that time were definitely not causing joy, and half dragged him out of the store . . . leaving a puddle behind.

Another thing Adam loved as a little boy was Charlene's father, his Pépère. Thank God she still had her father during those early years. More importantly, Adam had her father. He especially loved his Pépère's tractor and trucks. Once he retired from the shipyard, Pépère Routhier worked for Turgeon's Construction. He would bring Adam with him to the shop sometimes and teach him about the different trucks they used in the construction business. When one of Turgeon's trucks went by the house, Adam would yell out, "There goes number five!"

> *It made me feel good because I was always close to my dad when I was little. By the time I was a teenager, we argued all the time and drifted apart. I never really talked to him, so it's kind of funny that I always loved that in their relationship. Most of all, I knew Adam was in good hands when he was with my father. I knew he was safe. Even when Adam and Dad got separated from the rest of us on that train into Boston, everyone else was practically hysterical, but I knew Adam was safe.*

* * *

> *I know I'm the mother so you'll just think I'm prejudiced, but I have to say Adam did have incredible looks. I couldn't believe I had given birth to such a beautiful baby, and as he grew up it continued to amaze me that I had such a handsome child. Jenny was and still is beautiful but even she used to talk about what a good-looking boy he was. Smooth, unblemished skin. Straight, white teeth. A dimpled chin, brown eyes that matched his brown hair, cheeks that begged to be touched, and that smile . . .*

Good looks weren't all Adam had. He had a personality that just drew people to him. Friends, family members, they just wanted to be around him. Even as a little kid, he was fun and funny. One afternoon he was watching TV and a kids' show was on where a stick guy was running around in a stick box trying to get out of it. He ran, he jumped, he ran faster, trying to get out of that little stick box. Adam started laughing. And the faster the guy ran, the more frustrated he became—and the louder Adam laughed. Eventually Charlene started laughing too—at how much *he* was laughing.

Then there was the day—there were many of them, actually—when Adam was aggravating his sister. This particular day she had a friend over. He wasn't being mean exactly, just annoying. He'd scoot by and accidentally on purpose bump into her. He'd walk in and change the channel on the TV and then walk out of the room—after tossing the remote out of Jenny's reach, of course. He spilled a glass of juice and blamed it on her. He'd quietly but constantly mimic her and then deny he was doing it. The thing is, he adored Jenny, so Charlene finally asked him why he was bothering her so much. He said, "I have to. It's my job!" She shouldn't have, but Charlene couldn't help laughing at those words coming out of his perfectly serious face.

> *And I'll never forget the day we were in the car after I'd picked him up from school, and he comes out with, "Your mama is a llama!" I just burst out laughing as I drove. That had been the saying going around school that day. Then he got going on the Yo Mama jokes: "Yo mama's so stupid she thinks a quarterback is 25 cents change." "Yo mama's so fat, when she steps on the scale it says 'to be continued.'" "Yo mama's so stupid, she tripped over the cordless phone." "Yo mama's so ugly, she scares the crap out of the toilet." I finally had to make him stop because I thought I'd have an accident.*

* * *

> *I remember wondering every once in a while how I ever ended up the mother of such a child. He was so outgoing, so athletic, so handsome, so smart, so popular—so many things I wasn't—that I sometimes couldn't believe he was actually mine. I think maybe at times I was more like his number one fan than his mother.*

The thing is that, as he got older, Adam's personality and his good looks just got better. The day finally came when Charlene brought him to a girl's house for the first time. They didn't "go out" for very long—an interesting term when it comes to kids, since "going out" sort of implies actually going somewhere—but for Charlene it did signal the beginning of Adam growing up. She wasn't too upset when she found out they had broken up.

A short time later Adam started going out with a classmate named

Sarah. One afternoon Charlene arrived at school to pick Adam up from football practice. Sarah came out to the car and introduced herself as Adam's girlfriend. Sarah seemed nice and was very pretty. She was back in the foyer just inside the door when Adam came out of the locker room. Charlene watched the two of them hug, then Adam started out to the car. She was happy—she certainly wanted people to like him—but she was a little sad, too. By this time Jenny had gone off to college. Charlene could already see the day coming when Adam would be on his own—which meant so would she.

Eventually that relationship faded as well and, while he didn't offer many details, Adam and Sarah called it quits. Adam never really talked about his girlfriends with Charlene—what teenage boy wants to talk to his *mother* about girls. Still, sensing her parental responsibilities, Charlene did buy him a book at the Christian bookstore about adolescents growing up. It was all about the birds and bees, and she told him it was very important that he read it. He looked at her like, *I can't believe this is happening to me.* She never found out if he actually read the book, nor what happened to it. It just disappeared.

* * *

> *Don't think I'm stupid, though. Believe me, I knew my Adam was no angel. Oh, he was drop-dead handsome all right, and he was a great comedian. He had a way with words and, as he got older, he had a way with girls—but he was no angel.*

After Charlene's father died she and the kids moved back in with her mother so Mémère wouldn't be alone. Adam started going to Maplewood Elementary School in Somersworth and Jenny went to St. Thomas Aquinas High School in Dover. Jenny had always done well in school. Adam, on the other hand . . . well, even though he had a big heart, he had his problems—at home *and* at school.

Charlene received a phone call at work one day from Adam's principal who told Charlene she needed to meet with her and Adam the next morning in her office before school started. Charlene discovered Adam had been tying some other children up with a rope on the playground. She saw Adam's eyes getting watery and then hers did as well. No one remembers the punishment he received but it wasn't as bad as how he punished himself. Adam wasn't always strong enough to make the right choices, but he was never proud of himself when he made the wrong ones. Charlene was already wondering if she should have been stronger when it came to discipline.

Another time, when Adam was in high school, a police officer came to the house and told Charlene that Adam was being charged with assault. She was surprised because Adam tended to make friends easily and his friends were all good kids. There was this one boy, though, they all picked on—including Adam. The officer had a lot to say, but Charlene stopped hearing when he said the boy's arm had lighter or match burns on it. Adam had to go to Juvenile Court where he pleaded guilty. He had to write a letter of apology to the boy and to his mother, and go through the Juvenile Diversion program run by the city. He also had to attend regular meetings and do some fifty hours of community service through the Public Works Department. Adam was ashamed that time, too. Charlene really didn't know what else to do—he was way too old to spank.

Sadly, that wasn't the last time Adam made poor choices that got him into trouble. The next time Charlene got a call from the police, it was from an officer in Newington, NH. Adam had been caught shoplifting a pair of socks from a shoe store in the Fox Run Mall. Charlene had to go to the Newington Police Station to pick him up. Yes, she knew Adam felt ashamed that time, too. He wouldn't look at her the whole time they were with the policeman. He had to appear in Portsmouth District Court and they were both worried he would have to go to jail. Actually, Charlene was way beyond worried. In the end, Adam was fortunate to get an empathetic judge. He talked to Adam like a human being. He even told him in open court that he, too, had shoplifted when he was a teenager. He said he had learned some hard but valuable lessons from the whole experience, went to law school, and eventually became a judge. Charlene and Adam were very relieved when they left the courtroom, but she wasn't happy. Neither was he.

Then there was the night Adam called his mother after he'd been caught by another police officer. At this point, he was fifteen or sixteen. He and a group of friends had been caught drinking in the woods. All the kids that were there that night, at least all the ones who got caught, had to appear in Dover District Court. Because of a snafu in the arresting process, the charges were eventually dismissed. Adam was ashamed of himself that time, too, but as usual, after the fact. Charlene kept hoping that something would make an impact on him, that someday he would feel the shame early, *before* he did something that got him into trouble.

Chapter 3: Jenny

Adam was my brother, which meant he was also my sometimes friend, occasional confidant, and constant rival. I remember my mom being pregnant with Adam. I was somewhere between five and six at the time and didn't understand what it meant that Mom's belly was so big. We lived on Stewart Avenue in a second-floor two-bedroom apartment. The day he was born I was at daycare and when it was time to leave someone else came to pick me up to go see my new brother. Adam was born at Wentworth Douglas Hospital in Dover and Joe, his father, was there. The only reason I know that is because I can still remember a box of blue cigars he was passing around.

Jenny says her mother met Joe while she was on a camping trip with her cousin, and while she's sure there must have been some good moments, mostly what she remembers is the trauma. She was afraid of him. She's pretty sure he used drugs and she *knows* he drank—a lot. She argued with her mother over and over to end her relationship with him.

One night Jenny and Charlene came home to find Joe passed out in front of their apartment. They had to call an ambulance to come get him. Another time he barricaded them inside their apartment. There was another incident where he actually took off with Adam for several days. Adam was just a baby at the time and Charlene was frantic. It was around that same time when Joe got mad about something while he was drunk and destroyed a lot of things in the apartment. They returned home one night to find everything in shambles and all kinds of things, including Adam's baby pictures and birth certificate, torn up and strewn around the floor.

To make their situation even worse, Charlene was developing that new coping strategy of hers. She began drinking pretty heavily, sometimes sitting at the kitchen sink with a bottle of Bacardi, drinking until she passed out. Jenny often put Adam to bed. On nights when she was really scared she called her grandmother, who'd come over to wake her mom up. Those weren't good days, and to Jenny it seemed like they'd go on forever, like there would be no end. She vividly remembers breathing a long sigh of relief when Charlene finally got rid of Joe. Slowly her fears began to go away.

Jenny and Adam were at the Big Bird Daycare in Rochester when Adam took his first steps. Since she and her mother had been working hard at home to help him, she was really excited and proud to be a part of that moment. In fact, she actually felt a little sad for Charlene that she hadn't been there to see it.

> *I sort of started playing the role of a child parent beginning at about age six. Once Adam learned to walk there was no stopping him. He used to love wearing these rubber winter boots—all the time! He'd run around our apartment in his diaper and boots. Sometimes he'd sit in a laundry basket that I had tied a string to, and I'd pull him around the apartment. Other times he'd ride his John Deere tractor/bike that my Pépère had given him for Christmas.*

One way or another, Adam was on the go. Jenny tried hard to play her parent role, but really, for the most part, all she could do was go along for the ride—and what a ride it was.

* * *

> *Adam graduated from kindergarten at the daycare center in Somersworth. Mom, Mémère, Pépère and I attended. All the kids looked so cute in their little graduation caps. Adam brought my mom a carnation and gave her a hug and a kiss. He was so proud. I still remember the smile he had that day as he wrapped his arms around her.*

Not too long after Adam began first grade Charlene met Warren.

Warren worked with Mémère at some cleaning company. He had two children, Kevin and Jason, and he split custody with his ex-wife. The boys visited every other weekend. This was a happy time for Adam. He really enjoyed having two brothers, even if it was only twice a month. They all moved to an apartment in Rochester to begin a new life.

Eventually Warren wanted to get married. Charlene said "yes," and they began planning a wedding. A few weeks before the wedding Charlene's family threw her a surprise shower. Jenny was at her father's house and didn't know it was going on. Adam had been at his babysitter's house earlier that day and had been bitten by a dog. The bite was on his ear, so every picture of him at the shower features a little boy with a bandage around his head.

Unfortunately Charlene and Warren also fought quite a bit but it was usually small stuff. Eventually, they were able to put pettiness aside and finally got married at Charlene's sister's house in Exeter in August of 1990. Every once in a great while Jenny still watches the home video they shot of the big day. Her mother looked so pretty and so happy—at least for the day. For a time, she and Adam were happy, too.

Jenny was in the sixth grade, which would have made Adam five or six, when they both fell in love with professional wrestling and the WWF. Don't ask why—she'll tell you she has no idea. Adam even had a costume of one of the tag team brothers. He used to wear it around the house and make the face like they did on TV, sort of squinty eyes and a rectangular shaped open mouth with his lips pulled back over his teeth. He often tried to add a scary roar, but coming from a six-year-old it didn't sound very scary.

Adam also loved the Ninja Turtles. One Thanksgiving the whole family went to see the second movie, *Secret of the Ooze*. That might have been the beginning of what turned into one of their favorite things to do together: watch movies. They once rented *Cool as Ice* and watched it ten or twelve times before they had to return it to the video store the next day.

Then came the day Jenny literally scarred Adam for life. She was babysitting him one afternoon, either a snow day from school or a day during the summer. As a joke she snuck up on him, yelled really loudly, scared the crap out of him, and watched as he slipped and fell on the bathroom floor. He ended up with a permanent scar on his bottom lip. She still feels ashamed about that.

I remember the darndest things about myself and Adam when we were young. Like I remember the first Christmas present he ever gave me. What made it special was that he didn't have presents for anyone else that year, just me. It was a red Rugrats watch, one of those collectable items from Burger King. It could have been a stick of gum or a pipe cleaner bracelet. I didn't care because it was from my brother. I still have it.

* * *

When Jenny was in junior high school she, Adam, Charlene, and Meme (Charlene's mom, Jenny and Adam's grandmother) took a trip to Salem, Massachusetts, for the Haunted Happenings. It was the first "family vacation" they had all taken together. They stayed overnight at the Hawthorne Hotel and visited the House of the Seven Gables, the Pirate Museum, the Salem Witch Museum, and the site of the Salem Witch trials. The Pirate Museum was Adam's favorite—what six-year-old would not be fascinated with the likes of the patch-eyed, rum-drinking, treasure-hunting Captain Hooks of old. They also visited a wax museum, and even attended a reenactment of a witch trial. Adam could hardly sit still wondering if they were really going to burn the witch-woman at the stake.

One summer just after Adam had entered middle school, he convinced his mother to let him go to a week-long basketball camp in Franklin, New Hampshire. It was the first time he was spending an entire week away from home—and away from Jenny—so she bought him a plant for his dorm room so he'd think about her. It was a really cheesy looking peace bus with a plant inside. Jenny also took the day off from work so she could drive him and his friends there. Their road trips had begun.

When I got my license at the age of sixteen, Adam was the first person I took in the car with me. I was so excited and wanted to share it with him. We drove to the bank. Yup, to the bank. I don't think I even had any banking to do—I just wanted to drive somewhere and I wanted to take him. How weird is that?

Their road trips did eventually get more exciting than a stop at the Citizen's Bank drive-up teller to change a ten dollar bill into a five and five ones. For three summers, beginning around July, 2000, she and Adam took trips together to Six Flags New England in Massachusetts. They each brought a friend and spent the entire day at the park. He loved the high-adrenaline rides. She was scared to death and would wait in line with them but then chicken out every time. She never made it onto the Cyclone *or* the Thunderbolt. Yeah, the trips did get more exciting, but some twenty years later, that silly peace bus planter is still sitting on Jenny's desk in her office.

* * *

When Jenny was nineteen or twenty (so Adam would have been thirteen or fourteen), their Uncle Jim and Aunt Sue came to visit during the summer. The year before when they had come to hike Mt. Washington Adam had desperately wanted to go with them, but they thought he was too young to keep up. They promised, however, that they'd come again and that the next time he could go with them. Well, the "next time" arrived, and this time Adam, Jenny, Uncle Jim, Aunt Sue, and Tante Faye all hiked up Lion's Head trail to the summit. The plan was that they would hike up and take one of the scheduled vans back down. It was a gorgeous day in early July and Adam was full of energy. The aunts were doing a great job but struggled to keep up. For a while Tante Faye wore the backpack with all of their food and supplies, but eventually Uncle Jim took over. The group ate lunch at Hermit Lake looking out over the ravine. Captivated by the many different textures and shades of green, highlighted by a glistening sun and accented by subtle movement from a gentle breeze, it was absolutely beautiful.

As young and energetic as he was, Adam did his best to keep the group motivated and moving but it wasn't easy. The aunts preferred a much more relaxed pace so it took them a *very* long time to reach the top, so long in fact that they missed the last van going down. Adam was all excited about having to hike back down, but there was no way they would have made it, at least not safely. Fortunately, Uncle Jim advocated for them—pleaded for them was more like it—and the officials arranged for an additional van to get them back to the base of the mountain.

Another summer trip took Adam, Jenny, Charlene, and Meme to

Old Orchard Beach, Maine for several days. Adam was in middle school, had enough energy for three kids, and was beginning to discover hormones—more specifically, girls. During the day they spent a lot of time on the beach, which Jenny and Adam loved, but evenings, hanging out with their mother and grandmother, got pretty boring, unless you find playing Bingo exciting.

One night, though, Uncle Dan, Tante Faye, and a couple of their friends came to visit and they hit the town—and the amusement park. They spent time on the pier and had their picture taken as a family in the mock jail. In the photo, Adam was wearing a sports jersey and hat, and he was pretending to drink from a bottle of Jack Daniels. They also bought a picture of them riding the roller coaster. They all looked hysterical, but Adam *was* hysterical. His face looked more like a caricature than his real self: his jaw dropped and his cheeks and hair peeled back from the speed of the ride and force of the wind. That night beat the heck out of Bingo!

* * *

Jenny was almost through college by the time Adam went into high school, which was when he really began acting out. He started drinking, smoking marijuana, and using inhalants—mostly computer duster. To support his drug and alcohol use, he was also stealing from the mall. Jenny received a phone call one day from her friend, Jay, telling her that Adam had been suspended from playing football because he'd been caught smoking pot. He let her know that the whole team was questioned and he had supported Adam for being honest. Jay said he'd told Adam that if he was honest he would do everything in his power to help him. Because Adam admitted to what he had done, he was only suspended instead of getting kicked off the team. Adam blew it all off as "no big deal," but Jenny knew that playing football was, in fact, a *very* big deal to him.

> *Sometimes Adam would call me late at night when things weren't going so well with my mom. She never seemed to understand how her drinking affected us, how it took her away from us. She'd spend hours in the*

basement or outside in the garage. We'd want to talk but she just wasn't available. I can't remember the specific events of the incident but it was one of those phone calls—Adam on the other end, late at night, tearful and asking me why I left him? The pain this one question still causes me is almost unbearable. The truth is I needed to get away. I needed to get healthy. I remember telling him he could come and stay with me in Farmington (University of Maine Farmington). I knew it was something he would never do, leave his friends and Somersworth High. Whether or not we knew how unhealthy our mom was, we couldn't fully leave her. She needed us, and in our own way, we needed her, too. She was "Mom." She might not have been a rock, but she was ours. Yes, she struggled . . . with men and bills and booze, but she connected us . . . to home, to each other, to life.

Adam did go up and stay with Jenny one weekend while she was at UMF. Unfortunately she was not very proud of her actions during that visit. She knew all too well the negative impact alcohol had on her mother, but never realized (or maybe didn't want to realize) the message she was sending her brother by drinking herself. That weekend she hosted a keg party. For a while he hung out with them, drinking and doing keg stands, but eventually he went into the other room and played video games. Jenny discovered later on that he had other things on his mind.

One of the things Adam wanted to talk to his sister about was his father. Jenny knew Adam had been trying to find him; he'd confided that to her a few months before. So after that night of drinking she shared with Adam some of the things she knew about his father. She told him she never used any substances other than alcohol because his father had been heavily into drugs, which had scared the hell out of her. She also admitted to Adam that his father had been very abusive towards their mother.

Jenny didn't really want Adam's father involved in his life again, but she supported Adam trying to find him because she knew it was what she would do. She felt, though, like he needed to know some things about the man first. Jenny had done some research on the Internet and had found his most recent mailing address, which she gave to Adam.

> *In hindsight I feel guilty that I told Adam the negative things about his father, yet based on a letter I found on his computer, I guess he handled it okay. I'm glad. But to this day I want to kick myself for the negative example I set for him that weekend: that underage drinking is okay, that binge drinking is fun. I knew better and I'm ashamed I didn't do better. And that's not on him, or his father, or even our mother. That's on me.*

* * *

Jenny happened to be home the night of Adam's prom. She had made plans for the weekend but canceled them to help him get ready. He was going to the prom with a girl named Jordan. They left in a stretch limo for a fancy Italian dinner at Alexander's in Rollinsford. Charlene, Meme, and Jenny met them at the high school for the Grand March so they could take pictures. At one point Jenny found herself standing next to a girl Adam had gone out with once or twice the year before. Jenny overheard her talking to another girl and realized she was saying things about Adam—not very nice things. She heard her say that Adam had agreed to take her to the prom but then canceled to go with Jordan because Jordan, unlike her, was "going to put out." Being the protective big sister, Jenny really wanted to confront her but bit her tongue instead.

It was during that weekend that Adam told Jenny he was really struggling in school and that he might not graduate. He was missing work in most of his classes and had fallen so far behind that getting caught up seemed impossible. She knew how important graduating was to him and the possibility of it not happening was unacceptable. Jenny also knew that while her mother's intentions were always good, she lacked the motivation and persistence—and often the confidence—to see things through. She found it hard to be "parental" if it involved discipline or confrontation, particularly when it came to Adam. If the answers might be difficult, she tended to not ask the questions. So Jenny asked the questions: *What classes are you failing? Who are the teachers? What is the principal's name?* Before she left to go back to school, Jenny wrote a letter on Adam's behalf, advocating for—basically pleading for—whatever considerations and services he might need in order to graduate. She signed Charlene's name and sent it off.

> *I'll never forget the night my brother called me to tell me that he was going to be able to graduate after all. He thanked me for believing in him. His graduation day was one of the happiest days of my life. Thank God we took dozens of pictures! I came home for the weekend and spent it all with the family. I went to Piece of Cake, a party supply store, and bought every decoration imaginable—I even decorated his car. Sometime that Saturday afternoon I noticed he had a hickey on his neck. I asked about it just to tease him some. He said he "ran into a tree." I asked him what the tree's name was and he just gave me that sly half smirk/half smile.*

* * *

The night after graduation Charlene, Jenny, and Meme hosted a family party to celebrate. Adam could hardly wait to go through all the gifts he'd received and count up all the money. Ever the rivals, when he started gloating about all the cash he'd gotten, Jenny made a point of telling him that she got more money for her graduation because a lot more people had attended—it was a point she would regret making. In many ways Jenny was Adam's greatest advocate, but she also had a way of cutting him down like that, calling attention to areas where she thought she was better than he. She would tell him how unattractive he was, how she went to a private high school, how *average* he was. Mostly she was just playing around, teasing him. But partly, underneath, it was her childish way of trying to keep him in check, keep him from getting too full of himself.

Like when Adam first got his license. He wanted a car so badly. He tried and tried to convince his mother to help him get one. Money was usually tight for her and she was often behind on bills, but when it came to Adam she always went overboard—and don't think he didn't know that! Adam had to have the best of everything—and he got it: name brand clothes, the best cleats and football equipment. The boy was very much into his image. Clothes from Walmart? Not for Adam Routhier. Uh uh:

American Eagle, Aeropostal, Hollister. Somehow his mother always found a way to make it happen for him, and if she couldn't Meme made up the difference. One time Adam chipped his tooth during football practice. Charlene allowed him to stay home from school until she could get him to the dentist to have it repaired. You couldn't even tell anything had happened.

> *Truthfully, though, I was jealous of Adam, how good looking he really was and how popular he was. Wherever he went he made friends—without even trying. God, I wish I could take back some of the things I did and said. I wish we could go to the movies again. I'd even take him shopping. I'd give anything to be able to tell him how drop dead handsome I really thought he was.*

* * *

Early in August Jenny came home for a weekend. She and Adam spent all of Saturday together. For years movies had been their thing, and so they went to BarnZ's in Barrington and saw *Collateral Damage* with Arnold Schwarzenegger. Adam drove. Jenny still almost gets sick to her stomach reliving that trip to the theater, and she was equally scared the entire car ride home. He drove fast—really fast. Oh, he paid attention to the road and what was going on around him, but he was constantly riding the tail of the car in front of them, ever looking for a place to pass, ignoring any rights other drivers might have had. She tried telling herself that he was young, that this was just a phase he was going through, that all teenagers were like this, that eventually they outgrew it. She wishes she had yelled at him for speeding and driving reckless. She didn't. She doesn't remember doing much of anything except being scared and feeling relief when they finally got home.

The next morning, Jenny, Adam, and their mother went out for breakfast at the Gateway in Somersworth. They loved to go there after mass on Sundays for the buffet. They especially loved the home fries. Adam would eat home fries, bacon, and waffles. That was it. He didn't like eggs, and even though he ate like a horse, the boy never gained weight. That morning they reminisced about the time they'd been there as kids. Adam went to open up his syrup and spilled it all over himself.

They laughed about it all over again. A few hours later Jenny headed back to Farmington. That was the last time she saw him.

> *I talked to him on the 4th of September. I remember because Mom, Meme, and Aunt Carol were coming to Farmington to visit and they were late. I called home to vent and chat. Our family was always running late so he understood my frustrations. Looking back on it, I'm really glad they were late that time. Otherwise I wouldn't have called and talked to him. I wouldn't have had that last opportunity to say, "I love you." Thank God we always ended our conversations that way.*

Chapter 4: Mémère

Like most mothers, Mémère (Meme or Mems to most everybody) was concerned when she found out that her unmarried daughter was pregnant—it was not what she would have chosen for her. And, she was not wild about the father. But also like most mothers, Charlene was still her daughter. This wasn't about Meme, it was about her child and an innocent unborn baby—her soon-to-be newest grandchild.

Charlene had a C-section delivery when Adam was born, so he was a beautiful baby—none of that bright red pinched face that comes from trying to squeeze out through a super-tight birth canal. His color and shape were perfect and you just wanted to kiss his precious little cheeks constantly. When all of his hair came in it was very light except for one dark patch on the back of his head. It was so cute! Even as a tiny baby, people passing by while Charlene or Meme were out with him would say, "Watch out for that one, he's going to be a lady killer!" It would be quite a few years before they would find out just how right those passers-by were!

As a small child Adam particularly loved his Pépé, Meme's husband. He was only in his life for seven short years but they enjoyed a tight bond. Right after he retired from the Navy Yard, Pépé worked for Turgeon's Construction Company in Somersworth. Adam couldn't wait for Pépé to come home and take him for a ride in the "big tuck!" It didn't matter where they went or what they did. It could have been bringing a load of gravel to a house site in Durham or a load of crushed stone for a septic system in Berwick. He just couldn't wait for that ride.

Being good Roman Catholics, the ride on Sunday mornings was to church in the car. During Lent, Meme and Pépé went to Holy Rosary Church for mass and always brought Adam with them. They would usually meet Adam's Tante Grace who was a nun in the order of the Holy Cross. After mass the four of them would go the short distance to Burger King for a late breakfast/early lunch. Adam loved the time he spent with all three of them but, according to Meme, what he really loved was getting his Burger King crown.

It's funny the things you remember. Adam did indeed grow up into a handsome "lady killer" of a young man. In my mind, though, I will always see a beautiful little boy sitting with us at Burger King wearing a cardboard crown. And while I know he learned how to pronounce truck (probably in the first grade!), I swear I can still hear him saying "big tuck" all these years later.

* * *

One day Adam and Meme went to her other daughter's house, his Tante Faye's, in Exeter. Adam brought his friend Austin along. Faye and Meme loved to go antiquing, but mostly they just liked to shop and didn't really care where. The Exeter Handkerchief Factory specialized mainly in fabric, linens, and drapes, but they accessorized the store with antiques as well. On Meme's list of "needs" at the time was a new tea pot, and since the Handkerchief Factory had a tea room tucked into one section of their retail store, she figured that was a good place to look.

Of course, I wasn't real sure about bringing two young boys into a tea room. Given how rambunctious Adam was, even all by himself, the image of that "bull in a china shop" was playing all over my mind. But I talked to them on the way to Exeter about English "high tea," what it was and how refined English people served it. By the time I was done we were turning into Faye's driveway and she was waiting. I just sort of hoped my talk had made an impression—and I prayed a bit too.

They parked just down the street from the nineteenth-century factory buildings and the four of them walked up to the main entrance. It was in the front of a rather large but unimpressive building with big factory-style windows, usually in need of washing, and gray, weathered clapboards with white trim, always looking like they needed a good coat of paint. When you walked into the building you were greeted with huge displays of fabric in every pattern and color you could imagine, from upholstery cloth to dress material to formal linens and lace. There were living room settings, formal dining rooms, and bedroom suites, all of which included matching or complimentary window treatments. Meme and Faye had seen all this before, but the boys were amazed.

Once inside they made their way to the tea room where they found small, round tables with white linens and four chairs, set with English china teacups, saucers, and small plates along with antique silver flatware, tea pot, sugar and creamer. They chose a table with a lovely ornate curio cabinet beside it and a Queen Anne sideboard just behind. Each table was set differently and the walls were decorated with Victorian style paintings and portraits. It was like taking a short trip back in time.

Little did the boys know when they walked up to this big old building that they would be enjoying afternoon high tea, complete with cucumber sandwiches, freshly baked scones, and elegant French pastries, not to mention dozens of flavors of gourmet teas to which they could add sugar lumps or honey along with fresh lemon wedges.

> *I did find a new tea pot but the best part of the afternoon was watching Adam and Austin enjoying themselves, sashaying around that store while playing the part of English gentlemen. They even held their pinkies out while sipping their tea. I think of that day every time I go to Exeter to see Faye.*

* * *

There is no way to quantify how much Meme adored her grandson. She loved him for his smile, his laugh, and his sense of humor. She loved him for his hugs and his neatness, even for all the times he drove her to distraction, and those times got more frequent and more serious as he got older.

> *When it all started I think he thought I was stupid—or maybe just too old to know anything—but it didn't take long for me to figure out that he and his friends were smoking marijuana in his bedroom. After I put a stop to that, he thought moving it into the closet was going to*

throw me off. Maybe I should have just called the police, but I didn't have the heart to. He finally moved it out to the garage and I just didn't have the energy to fight it anymore. He probably thought I never figured that out. I'll tell you, the whole marijuana thing made me wish for a return to the days when my biggest problem with Adam was getting him to go to mass—and stay in mass. He probably thought I never figured that out either!

Adam had his sweet side, though, and it was more than just his smile. One time he decided to cook dinner for his girlfriend Brittany. It was her birthday and he wanted to do something really special for her. The only problem was that Adam was no great cook, at least if it meant going much beyond boiling water for ramen noodles or hot dogs. And baking? Forget about it. So he made mac and cheese, and served it on Meme's best china—with a candle. Yes, there were times when Adam embodied the lazy "dumb jock," but that wasn't one of them.

By the time he was sixteen he must have decided he needed to do better than mac and cheese, because for Valentine's Day he actually cooked and served Brittany a beautiful three-course dinner, complete with candlelight and soft music.

For all of his struggles, my Adam was definitely a romantic at heart! Brittany was a nice girl, too—good for Adam. I was sorry to find out they had broken up.

Chapter 5: Tante Faye

When Adam was little he spent quite a lot of time in Exeter where his aunt and uncle lived with their kids: Tante Faye, Oncle Ken, and cousins Jamie, Ron, and Paul. Birthday parties were usually spent at Meme and Pépé's house in Somersworth, but almost all of the major holidays were spent in Exeter. Adam loved to play with his cousins and his sister. Faye and Ken had quite a lot of land, and a pond where the kids spent hours skipping stones, running around, and splashing each other.

One of Adam's favorite things to do in the summer was catch frogs. He and the other kids would run around that pond with nets and try to catch as many frogs as they could. In the winter they couldn't wait to to ice skate, throw snowballs, and build snowmen.

Another thing they loved to play was ninja warriors. Once it started to get dark outside, they'd all put on black clothes and run around the property pretending they were ninjas. They would eventually move inside to spy on all the adults as they sat around drinking coffee and chit-chatting. You never knew when some kid was going to jump out with a full-blown, heart-attack yell—in arms-straight-out, feet-planted, knees-bent full ninja attack stance. It was hysterical.

And eat—could those kids eat! One of the things Adam especially loved was cantaloupe. If the whole family was over and Tante Faye was going to serve cantaloupe at meal time she'd buy two, or even three if they were small, because Adam would literally eat an entire one by himself. And Campbell's Chicken Noodle Soup. No way anybody was going to trick Adam with any of that homemade stuff. Nope, it had to be "real" chicken noodle soup.

I guess what I remember most from those years was how much Adam loved just being at my house. He loved playing with his cousins. My parents' house in Somersworth was an in-town location, so he loved being able to play outside and run around when he visited us.

He loved coming and he hated going—it was usually a pretty tearful good-bye.

* * *

Truth be told, Tante Faye enjoyed having Adam around almost as much as he enjoyed being around. He was simply a lot of fun, even when he was getting a little older. Adam's Oncle Ken was the chief of police in a small neighboring town. Every year the police department hosted a big Halloween party. Adam sometimes brought friends to the huge event. He often invited Steven, Ty, and DJ, and some years would include Austin and Jake, too. There were probably others as well—he did have a lot of friends, and being very active boys, they knew how to have fun—too much fun sometimes! No one could keep track of them all, so basically no one tried. They just ran from booth to booth trying to win prizes, scavenging as much candy as they could find, and, if they thought they could get away with it, sometimes even trying to grab what other kids had found.

Honestly, Adam was such a hoot to be around, whether it was at my house or my mother's in Somersworth. When I visited there, even if he didn't happen to be around, I still got to hear all the latest Adam stories. For example, it was very common for Adam to have friends sleep over on the weekends, so my mother would make the boys her special pancakes and waffles. She figured out how many to make by counting the sneakers on the floor by the door. Doesn't sound much like a kid thing to do, but Adam would make his friends take their sneakers off when they came into the house, just like he did.

Oh yes, Adam may have been a kid but he was also Mr. Clean. He showered at least twice a day, most days more. He would scrub his hands so much they were usually bright red. He was always having to lather them with hand lotion. And it seemed like he was constantly changing his clothes. Mem washed and ironed daily just for him. She even ironed his friends' clothes! One time Austin had left a bunch of his clothes in Adam's room. Mem thought they were Adam's clothes that he had outgrown, so when Austin went to get them he discovered they had been sent to the Salvation Army, since they were much too small for Adam!

Then there was the time . . . while driving back to New Hampshire with Tante Faye, Adam became very inquisitive. He must have been nine or ten years old at the time, and he started asking questions about dogs and cats. At first it was things like, *Can dogs get married?* and *How do they have puppies?* and *What about cats and kittens?* Then he started asking about people and how babies were made. He'd obviously been hearing something about sex, had lots of questions, and was very insistent on getting truthful answers. There was no getting away with the stork delivery stuff; Adam wanted the facts. Faye did her best, even though in the back of her mind she was thinking, *Wait a minute, I'm just the aunt here!*

* * *

Fay got a kick out of the fact that Adam loved weird stuff—well maybe not "weird" but different. One of the places he loved was Logan Airport. Now most people who have to use it tend to hate Logan Airport. Just getting there from New Hampshire is an aggravation. Driving in and around Boston is an absolute nightmare. And once you're there, try finding a place to park—at least a place that doesn't cost enough to require a second mortgage on your house! Anyway, one time he'd gone with Faye to drop off Oncle Jim for his flight back to Texas. Since they didn't often brave Boston, Tante Faye thought it would be fun to do a little sight-seeing in the city and then have a nice Italian lunch at Pauli's in the North End. Later, after they arrived back home, his mother asked him what he liked best in Boston. His answer? Logan Airport.

The thing that most fascinated him about Logan was all the people coming and going. He couldn't get over the long lines at the ticket counters, the traffic jams caused by travelers, baggage handlers, and luggage carts—and the constant flow of men, women, and children on stairs, escalators and elevators. He really didn't want to leave.

Then there was Faye's dog. Adam just loved Rosie. Nobody really understood why. After all, Adam was this strapping, muscular boy and Rosie was a little dachshund that probably would have fit into a slightly oversized coat pocket, but he loved that dog. Rosie even went to a few of his football games during his freshman and sophomore years at Somersworth High. Airport traffic, crowds, and little dogs—go figure!

* * *

Some might think it odd or accuse her of being in denial, but Tante Faye never wanted to hear or think about any bad things when it came to her nephew. Oh, she knew Adam got himself into a lot of trouble, but she always wanted to think about his good qualities. Even after the accident—she just didn't want to remember him that way. And so she decided to remember only the good things, the fun things, like the time Adam was taking driver's ed during the summer of 2002.

Tante Faye and Oncle Ken had recently moved into a new place in Hampton, and Adam spent quite a lot of time with them. He had a crush on Christine and Brittany, two girls who were visiting from Florida. All the kids were in driver's education classes but no one was actually driving yet, so Faye got to be the chauffeur. One evening she took the kids out to a nice dinner in downtown Exeter and then to a movie. Adam really turn on his charm–-always smiling, opening doors, and pulling out chairs. Faye characterized it as *unbelievable*.

Downstairs at their house, Faye had a big game room with a pool table and wide-screen TV. The kids all spent the weekend together which meant that Tante never got a minute's sleep. No way was she going to leave Adam downstairs alone with the two beautiful Florida girls.

Another night Tante Faye served Adam and the girls a special dinner on the back deck, with candles and sparkling water. She even used her good dishes. Chicken parmesan, tossed salad, garlic bread, and brownie sundaes for desert. Adam ate enough for everyone, while the girls picked at a few bites. After all, they had to watch their figures.

I certainly know Adam had his problems, and I know how horrific the accident was. I know how ridiculously fast he must have been going for it to have . . . I just don't want to remember him that way—and I'm not going to.

Chapter 6: Oncle Jim

The Texas branch of the family (Charlene and Faye's brother, wife, and kids) only saw Adam once or twice a year, so their collective memories of him as a baby are pretty thin. They do have photos, though, and have gone through them many times over the last ten years. Each one remembers him as a very cute baby and quite the curious toddler. Oncle Jim vividly remembers how much Adam loved his Pépé's John Deere tractor. Jim says, "I can see him now, twenty-plus years later, sitting on that tractor pretending to drive it."

> *There is one memory that stands out strongly. On a visit to New Hampshire in 1991, my mom and dad, sisters Charlene and Faye, and our families drove to the Wonderland "T" station near Revere Beach on the North Shore where we were going to catch a train into Boston, planning to spend the day there. We were still in the process of buying everyone tickets when my father, who kept stressing that we all needed to stay together, saw a train coming into the station. Dad, who must have already had his and Adam's tickets, said, "Here's the train!" He grabbed five-year-old Adam's hand and got on. The problem was, the rest of us didn't have our tickets. We were screaming for him to get off the train when suddenly the doors closed and he and Adam were stuck on board. I will never forget the looks on their faces: Dad's, knowing he had messed up, was a cross between sheepish and guilty, while Adam, so small and innocent, just stood there holding Dad's hand looking like everything was fine. The rest of us were sort of freaking out—especially my son, who was convinced he would never see his cousin and Pépé again.*

Of course no one had cell phones in those days, but it all worked out. The ticket agent called the next station and had them get off there. Everyone else met them at the Revere Beach Station, a short distance away, went on to Boston and had a great day of sight-seeing. They saw North Church, walked a lot of Paul Revere's trail, and had lunch at Quincy Market's Faneuil Hall Marketplace—them and maybe ten thousand others! The favorite stop, though, was "Old Ironsides." Adam was beyond excited to be on a military boat. They were able to take the guided tour, so everyone got to go below deck and see where the sailors had lived and worked some two hundred years before. Of course, Adam didn't quite understand why he couldn't walk under the two-inch thick rope cordoning off the Revolutionary era cannons and why he couldn't lie down in one of the bunks—which looked more like hammocks than bunks. Still, he had a great time and wasn't bothered at all by the unscheduled start. Actually, it's doubtful he ever even realized anything had gone wrong.

* * *

With one son in college and another in high school in Texas, Jim and his family didn't have a lot of contact with Adam for a few years. Adam did, however, come out to stay with them for a few days just after his freshman year in high school. Jim's son Joe and his fiancé Amber were graduating from the University of Houston and Adam made the trip south with Meme. During their stay they visited the university campus and the Museum of Science. One Wednesday afternoon, May 9, 2001, Adam and Jim met up with Joe and Amber at Enron Field (now Minute Maid Park) to see the Astros take on the Phillies in the final game of the series.

The group got to the park early and Adam and Jim went into the Crawford boxes in left field to watch batting practice and try to snag some home runs. They came close (one ball hit about five seats to their left), but didn't manage to get a ball. Eventually they made their way up to the mezzanine where their seats were located. Being Astros fans, Jim and Joe were glad they could salvage something in that series—Houston avoided a sweep with a one-run squeaker of a win. Thank God both Jeff Bagwell and Lance Berkman hit home runs off Chen.

I can remember at some point during the game Joe

and Adam wrestled a little, threatening to throw each other to the seats below. Once the tussle started I think my son sensed some strength in Adam he'd never had before and decided to save face by ending the match. Shortly thereafter I overheard Joe say, "When did you become such a stud?" It occurred to me as I took a closer look at him that my not-so-long-ago little nephew with the impish smile and gelled hair was growing up.

The whole family met up again later that summer in Nebraska, when Joe and Amber were married. Adam was an usher in the wedding which took place at a small community church in Omaha. He wore a black tuxedo with a white shirt, black bow tie, and black patent leather shoes. He was a very handsome young man. Jim felt a great deal of pride watching him escort both Charlene and Meme down the aisle to their seats.

I remember noticing quite a few of the young girls there were checking him out. I'll bet they were pretty disappointed to discover he lived more than two thousand miles away!

Book Two

Mr. Mac and Friends

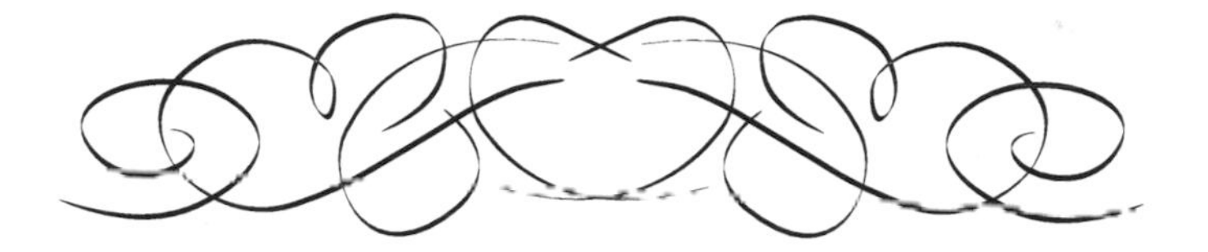

Chapter 1: Mr. Mac

Students often find it somewhat strange to run into their teachers outside of school, like at the mall or Home Depot or the grocery store. They must think teachers don't have lives outside of school—maybe even that they don't exist beyond the boundaries of the school yard. Yet, Adam and this group of kids always maintained that they first "met" me at Cumberland Farms.

Living in the city in which I teach, I run into students and former students all the time in all kinds of places: Walmart, Target, Burger King, and Market Basket. Of course I don't just run into them in Somersworth. I frequently run into students at the Fox Run Mall, even the Mall of New Hampshire in Manchester. Believe it or not, I actually ran into a student once in the Miami Airport.

I kind of enjoy it. I like for my students to know I have a life, that I have to buy groceries, grass seed, and 2 x 4s like everybody else. I like them to see that I don't treat them any differently outside of school than inside. And I especially like it when I run into a kid with whom I have had, or maybe even am having, a problem. I like them to realize that I don't hold grudges, that every day is a brand new day, that their problem with me (or mine with them) as a student does not affect how I see them as a person.

Several of these particular kids engaged in behaviors I definitely don't approve of, and they engaged in them on a regular basis. I didn't like *it*, but I still loved *them*. Knowing that is probably why Adam felt like he could come to me when this "behavior" began to control his life. Family doesn't stop being family just because individual members disappoint us.

Most days I begin my classes with a *question of the day*. One of those is *What do you believe in?* That's it. *What do you believe in?* I don't give any hint of any direction in which to take their answer. I usually get a few "ghosts," "friends," and "God." One time a student said, "I believe in second chances." "Wow!" I replied, "Me too . . . and third and fourth and fifth chances," if I feel like someone's request is sincere.

A colleague of mine—a pretty close one—was telling me one day about a problem he was having with Adam's friend, Joey. Joey had made a remark that afternoon in the hallway that was grossly inappropriate and blatantly disrespectful. The colleague said, "Oh, he apologized but I didn't accept his apology." I replied, "What do you mean, you didn't accept his apology? You have to accept it!" He commented back, "I disagree. I think sometimes there have to be consequences." I immediately responded, "Who said there didn't. Of course there have to be consequences. But if a student, or anybody else for that matter, wrongs you what other recourse do they have than to apologize? I mean, what else can they do? And if you don't accept their apology, doesn't that say more about you than it does about them?"

The next day the colleague made a point of stopping by my room to tell me that he'd worked everything out with Joey and they'd shaken hands. "Great," I replied. "What happened to get you there?" "Well," he said, "Joey came in this morning and apologized *again*, and I felt like he meant it . . . and . . . I thought a little more about what you said."

Every year on the first day of school, I go over a litany of things that my new students can and should expect when it comes to me and my classroom. Yes, the list includes the normal and the mundane: *get to class on time, do your homework, treat each other with respect, don't laugh at other people in our classroom when they make a mistake*, that kind of stuff. But one of the most important things on my list is this: *You need to understand something. You're one of mine now, and what that means is that for the rest of our lives you will never again not be one of mine*.

We also go over the syllabus, which details the content of the course, major literature and papers, the schedule of assignments, due dates and the like. It also includes classroom policies and expectations regarding things like homework, behavior, make-up work, etc. But the most important thing in my syllabus is this paragraph:

> *One final thought. If you earn an "F" in this class you will have failed the course—and that will be sad. If you leave this classroom not knowing that I love you and value you, then I will have failed you—and that will be tragic.*

Technically speaking *I* am the teacher in my classroom, but that is just one of the many things Adam Routhier taught *me*.

Chapter 2: Steven

I was Adam's best friend. I met him for the first time in third grade, 1995, but in fourth grade we had the same teacher, Mr. Ready, and that's when we really became friends. From then on we were more like brothers. He could make me so happy at times, and then there were other times I'd want to wring his goddamn neck . . . haha. We were both very strong willed, confident, and rarely wanted to admit any faults or, God forbid, being wrong. So, naturally heated discussions and arguments would erupt from time to time, like who was better at football, who was the superior Madden player, who could get the hottest chicks.

Because Adam grew up without a father, friends were an important part of his life. That's probably why when we were growing up, his house was always filled with his friends. Adam was extremely social. It's one of the reasons he was such a special kid and people wanted to be friends with him. He would actively try to make his friends laugh and genuinely enjoyed making them happy. He was a smart, loyal, funny, goody-two-shoes, charming, authentic, rebellious, adventurous, confident, cocky, hurt, hurtful, misguided, thoughtful, introspective, athletic, insulting, caring guy. He was a daredevil and a dick-head. He was so goddamned compulsive at times but kind and compassionate at others. Most of the time I would have told you I loved him—well, I probably wouldn't have told you that but I did. But there were times, usually only moments, when I loathed him. Like the night he tore my life to shreds for close to two years—but I'll save that for later.

Right now I want to tell you about the joke we pulled on Mr. Ready when he was filling in as assistant principal at Maplewood Elementary. I believe our substitute teacher got the idea to have a little surprise birthday party for Mr. Ready. To get him down to the classroom, the teacher called the office and said that Adam had acted up and thrown a chair across the room. This was totally believable because Adam had a tendency to act up. Whether he was annoying other kids on the playground, taking somebody down on the Tire-Tanic so he could be first to the top, stealing another kid's book, hiding someone's lunch, or just finding a way to disrupt the class, he was certainly viewed as a troublemaker by Mr. Ready.

So we turned a chair upside down, placed it so it was easily seen as soon as anyone came through the door, and waited. It didn't take long for Mr. Ready to come storming into the room, his beet red face showing his anger. "Adam Routhier," he hollered, "what have you done now?" Adam, with a guilty look on his face, didn't have a chance to answer because the class burst out in a chorus of "Happy Birthday!" We all died laughing—including Mr. Ready. A funny moment made possible by Adam's reputation.

* * *

The thing about Adam was that Steven didn't have to pretend. If they were doing something together they could both play to win, and no matter which one of them did, they were still friends afterwards, at least within a few minutes. Like when they first met in the fourth grade and Mr. Ready used his multiplication flashcards. Steven always wanted to win and he knew Adam was his main competition—and Adam knew Steven was his. The game had two lines that faced Mr. Ready. He'd pull a flash card and the first person at the head of the two lines who answered correctly won. Both players then went to the back of the opposite line. The neat thing was they kept getting paired up against different classmates. Mr. Ready praised the kids who were doing well, so it would get pretty competitive. The smarter kids could do the higher parts of the tables whereas the others couldn't. It became a fun way to want to learn the times tables and kids got a chance to go against their friends. It didn't always come down to Adam or Steven, but often it did, and neither one of them liked losing.

There were a lot of links that developed between those two. They both loved their sports, especially football, played way too many video games, and had the same weird sense of humor. Each of them also had a wicked mischievous streak. The first time Steven went to Adam's house he discovered what would become his second home: Adam's room. It was big and there was no carpet yet, so they were able to toss a tennis ball off the walls and wood floors. Throwing a ball *indoors*! A new friendship had begun.

By the time they got into middle school Steven would sleep over at Adam's house nearly every weekend. Sometimes, with a little extra pleading, his mother would let him stay both Friday *and* Saturday nights. They would stay up way too late playing Madden and watching movies, waiting for Charlene to go to bed so they could watch the smut shows on Showtime After 12. Adam also had this game called Resident Evil, an extremely gory and scary video game with zombies. Steven would read the strategy guide to help Adam as he worked his way through it—because he was too scared to actually play the darn thing himself! They would turn all the lights off and play the game at night. There was this place in the game that was the absolute scariest. It always made Steven jump, so one time when it was coming up Adam yelled right in Steven's face. Steven jumped in his seat and, turning quickly away from Adam, slammed his face off the vertical bar holding up the old red bunk bed. They both laughed like crazy, even though Steven thought he'd busted his nose!

Usually on Saturday mornings Adam and I would get up and drink a Carnation Instant Breakfast. We didn't have that at my house. And then we'd set out on our day. We'd often go across the street to hang out with the Drews. We used to play football in their yard a lot. Usually Austin, Andy, Kenny Head and some others would join in. We had a blast playing those games. Sometimes they ended with a Josh Drew meltdown where he wanted to kill his older brother. Other times we'd play until somebody got hurt, like by an Adam tackle, started crying, and went home.

If they didn't play football they'd go down to the sand pits by Russell Stover's, or into the woods behind the Drews' house. They usually weren't really bad, but they did like seeing how much trouble they could cause without getting caught—breaking off tree branches, throwing rocks, lighting little fires, basically kid stuff. Adam really looked up to the Drews and was proud to show off Steven and his other friends from school to his cool, older neighbors. He was always trying to impress them. One time they went out to a field just beyond the woods and set off a toy rocket ship Chris Drew had gotten from Walmart. They were beyond pleased with themselves over that one

The other thing we loved to do was ride our bikes. We all had BMX bicycles and we rode them for hours at a time. We went all over town, to the middle school, the sand pits, Cumby's. We'd even ride all the way to South Berwick sometimes. We used to race, play chicken, and dream up all kinds of tricks and stunts which could easily have ended with broken arms, broken legs, or broken necks for that matter. We were invincible. All of us, especially Adam, loved taking risks. He started this on-going competition to see who could leave the longest and darkest skid marks on the street in front of his house. And if we made a car stop while we were out there competing, well that was even better. Life was sweet.

Somewhere along the way Adam Routhier picked up a nickname: "Ruth." The sleep-overs at Ruth's continued, maybe even increased, as they got older. Saturday nights were always a tough sell because Steven had to convince his mother they were going to go to mass the next morning. Unfortunately, Meme was an avid churchgoer so it turned out he was rarely lying, or even stretching the truth. They would pretend to be sleeping Sunday morning, hoping Meme would just let them be, but she was a straight shooter . . . "I know you boys are awake," she'd holler. "Get up. We're going to mass!" Damn Meme, spoiling all the fun.

One time when he slept over things went a little sour. They went to church that next morning, the same one Steven's mother attended. They sat in the kids' "silent room" in the way back so they could leave after receiving communion. They knew Steven's mother would be watching to see them go up for communion, so once they ate the cardboard chips and started making their way back toward the silent room, they just kept going, out of church like a couple of rebels, and started walking to Adam's house. Steven's mother, who was nobody's fool and certainly not theirs, suspected the early departure and decided to drive home by a route similar to the one she knew they'd take walking to Adam's. She was some ticked off to find them so close to his house in such a short period of time. The next couple of Sundays found them attending the *whole* mass, and there were no Saturday night sleep-overs for a while.

> *Once the sleep-overs picked back up, though, we sort of became movie aficionados. We used to watch a ton of movies—and not just the after-midnight soft porn on HBO or Cinemax either. I still remember the first movie we went to see with each other at the theater. It was Broken Arrow in 1996. We use to act like we were Siskel and Ebert when it came to the big screen. After watching a movie we would critique it, analyze it, and do comparisons to other films. We were always quoting movies like dorks, whether in our away messages, on the phone, or in person. Some of our favorites were The Matrix, Gladiator, Point Break, Scarface and Goodfellas. "You take the blue pill—the story ends. You take the red pill—you stay in Wonderland." "You wanna fuck with me? Your fucking with the best!" "I always tell the truth. Even when I lie." Any Given Sunday… real classics.*

As much as they had in common, though, probably the thing that helped them become such close friends was the difference in their upbringings. They just felt at ease with each other. Adam didn't exactly envy the lack of freedom at Steven's house but he definitely envied the fact that Steven had his mother *and* his father. And even though *both* of Steven's parents were ex-military, way stricter than Charlene, Steven knew they were good parents and was some thankful he had them.

Still, Adam's house was way more lax when it came to discipline, and I don't know many kids who don't like that. I felt comfortable over there, like I could totally be myself. I could rebel a little, be a little badder.

* * *

By freshman year of high school the big red bunk bed was gone but they were still having sleep-overs, sometimes literally piling people into Adam's room. Steven, Austin, Jake and others. Austin, that sketch, always seemed to leave before anyone else got up and would leave his dirty socks . . . the wacko. It gave them a laugh, though.

Austin started a weird tradition, too. I still remember the first time he did it. One afternoon after hanging out for a while in Ruth's room, Austin left to go home. Then about ten minutes later from the bottom of the stairs he yells, "I struck again!" We'd look at each other like, "What the fuck is he talking about?" Shortly thereafter I go to the bathroom to find a lone turd in the toilet. I yelled to Ruth to come look. This is what the fucker meant! The weirdest part was there wasn't any toilet paper in the bowl. That was one of the many pranks we pulled on Ruth. As disgusting as it was, I struck a few times too.

The bunch of them were always looking for new ways to push, stretch, and test the limits. Adam's desktop computer was outside his room upstairs, so they were always pranking him on it. Like when they were leaving they'd open up his AOL instant messenger account and change his away message, leaving something like "I love men," or "Gone to whack off!"

Eventually the entire group of them began experimenting with weed in Adam's room. They'd pile people in there and smoke. One time Adam, Steven, Austin and Jared were all wrestling after getting high. The whole room was filled with smoke. What they did sometimes was take a sock off their foot, put in on their hand, and then try to stuff their hand into someone else's mouth while wrestling (inspired by the professional wrestler, Mankind). While they were raising a ruckus and being fools, the door to the room swung open and in walked Meme—pissed. She yelled at them about what was going on. It was pretty obvious as she looked at their bloodshot eyes, goofy smiles and the foggy air that they were high. Jared had left the room before Meme came in, so when she started accusing them of smoking pot, Adam responded by saying, "No, it was Jared. He's probably in the bathroom doing it right now." Meme wasn't falling for it. She yelled, "No! It was all of you!" Those words sent shivers down Steven's spine as he thought about what his parents would do if they found out. Smoking in the room stopped—at least when Meme was home.

This led to the infamous closet, which Adam had newly dubbed, "The Cudaberry Clizo," "Cudaberry" referring to a girl's anatomy and "Clizo" being a play closet. Thank Snoop Dogg, probably. He played on those kinds of words and may have even coined them, who knows. Anyway, they started sitting in the Cudaberry Clizo to smoke for a couple of reasons: One, to avoid flak from Meme. Two, sitting in an enclosed area tends to get you higher. It kind of became a favored hangout spot. It was a pretty big closet . . . and they loved the name!

> *We would sometimes pile three, four, five people in there. Ten years later I regret all the smoking, but I do fondly remember sitting in there with my friends and enjoying ourselves, having deep conversations about the meaning of life, philosophy, was there a God. And of course girls. I remember sometimes being in the Cudaberry Clizo and wishing I could freeze myself in the moment because of how happy I was.*

At that time, Adam didn't know if there was a God, but he believed there was a something. He had a mentality, as did Steven, that they were going to live life with no regrets. If they died, they died. They were going to be fearless and do what they wanted when they wanted.

> *I wish I could go back and shake that rubbish out of our heads. Part of it was because of our immaturity and the "invincibility" that came with it. But Ruth was a great*

talker and he loved to get all theoretical about that kind of stuff. Some days we were in there for hours just talking. Then we'd come stumbling out to play video games, watch movies, listen to music, and finally raid the kitchen.

Chapter 3: DJ

I was Adam's best friend. Adam was a passionate guy. Whether it was sports, video games, singing along to classic rock, or gelling his hair Adam showed a lust unequalled by his other friends, me included. If he liked something, he loved it. If he didn't love it, he didn't do it. He was also a hilarious kid. I never laughed so hard as I did when I was with him. Sometimes I'd start laughing before he actually did anything, just thinking about what he might do. Like you could tell from the way he dribbled the basketball that he was about to throw the ball up in some ridiculous way and I'd start laughing at the shot before he ever took it. Or the way he'd scream just before starting to wrestle one of his friends and my laughter would erupt as I pictured that first dive towards one of us.

DJ met Adam and his friend Austin the first day of third grade at Maplewood Elementary School. He was in a new classroom with a lot of new kids–-and a first year teacher no one knew anything about. DJ walked into the room thinking about the fact that all of his friends, especially Joey and Steven, were in other classes and here he was all by himself, and stuck with this new teacher as well. "This is gonna be so bad!" he thought. Boy, was he wrong.

Like any good first-year teacher, she had everyone sit in a circle to do class introductions. DJ was extremely nervous because he literally didn't know anyone and his first impression of the teacher was that she seemed pretty strict. Everyone was being shy and looking down a lot until the teacher introduced herself. She said her name was Mrs. Crockett. Right away Adam asked what her first name was. She smiled politely and replied, "Sandy." Then Adam, without another word, started singing, "San-dy, San-dy Crockett, king of the wild frontier." DJ had never heard the song, didn't know what it was from, and yet he couldn't control himself. The whole class burst into laughter. Even Mrs. Crockett was smiling.

Maybe, though, one of the things I most admired about Ruth was his honesty. He was never afraid to say what was on his mind or share his feelings. He expressed himself every day in every way and didn't care if others liked it or not—sometimes to a fault, but not usually. If he didn't like someone, everybody knew it—including the person he didn't like. You didn't want to take your shoes off when you went into his house, you didn't go into his house. You didn't like losing at Madden, you did not play Ruth. You didn't like the fact that he had to have his T-shirts, polo shirts, even his boxers ironed along with his jeans, khakis, and dress shirts—too fuckin' bad.

A lot of Adam's idiosyncrasies seemed weird to his friends, and by their own admission he could be an obnoxious prick, but you never had to wonder what he thought or where you stood with him. You know what else? Twenty-something years later, DJ still hasn't seen the movie or read the books, and couldn't tell you one thing about Davy Crockett, the real "king of the wild frontier," but that's irrelevant. That song was the unofficial theme song of his third grade year, and it will get replayed in his head until the day he dies.

One thing I always remember is Ruth being extremely talented in his ability to figure out math problems way faster than the other kids. Third grade math: I don't even remember what the content was, but Adam was always the fastest in the class, lightning fast, when it came to arithmetic stuff. Some kids would use the charts and cheat sheets and tables to work out their solutions. Not Adam. He always had a unique way of figuring out his problems. And when I say lightning quick, I mean like Back to the Future lightning quick. Ruth would be finished with his math quizzes about the time most of us finished putting our names on them. Whether he had his times tables memorized or he could just fly through them at warp speed I don't know, but I do know he helped me understand a way to do math quickly. I can't give you an exact problem–third grade was a long time ago. But try this as an example of the way he thought at a young age: Let's say the problem was 9 x 8 + 98. I would get out my pencil and paper, figure out the multiplication, then add that answer to the 98 the long way, carrying the one, etc., while Ruth would see 72 + 100 – 2 = 170 almost instantly. When he told me that he'd simply round everything up and then minus the difference, I thought it was the math equivalent of rocket science. Work smarter, not harder. I guess the larger point, though, is that Ruth just had this ability to solve things. Even when he was nine years old, he saw things differently than most of the rest of us. He could just sort of simplify life and find solutions . . . his way . . . fast.

Doing things his way was one of Adam's most valued trademarks. He and DJ were in the same class in the sixth grade. They had Mrs. Hodgson, who had just won the Walmart Teacher of the State award, and Ms. Madiriaga, who taught math, was strict, and loved the Denver Broncos, a topic she and Adam would frequently talk about. One of the assignments for social studies that year was a three-week project requiring all the kids to partner up and construct a castle which had to meet a detailed list of requirements. Rule #1 was that the parents should not be helping, but when it came time to turn in the finished projects it was obvious which kids, and parents, had abided by Rule #1. Clearly Adam and DJ had received no parental help whatsoever. Adam was way too stubborn to ask, and DJ was way too chicken to go against him. And true to form, for Adam anyway, they waited until the last possible minute to start, completing the entire castle over the two-day weekend before it was due.

They used whatever they could find around the house: old cardboard boxes, cups, plastic ware, spray paint, construction paper, toilet paper rolls, markers. DJ claims it was one of the worst assignments he has ever submitted. It was haggard. They used an extra-large plastic cup for the center of the castle, and glued it to a big piece of flat brown corrugated cardboard. Their castle didn't have a grassy courtyard. It didn't have cobblestone walkways or realistic looking plastic trees and shrubs from

Ben Franklin crafts. It didn't have inset doors and shutters. No, their doors and windows were drawn on with a black marker. Their moat was simply a white paper ring around the entire castle about five inches wide and colored with blue magic-marker. Their drawbridge was a collection of used Popsicle sticks hurriedly glued together. You didn't even have to look very hard to see the light hues of red, blue, and green from the Popsicles they'd held not long ago.

Now one might think, *well, that doesn't sound like it was too bad; at least it seems like it was in keeping with the assignment*. Well, one castle actually had a moat made out of gray modeling clay with running water. One was built entirely out of Legos that had been spray-painted light brown. Another one had a *working* drawbridge, with real chains. None of this fazed Adam. DJ was embarrassed to bring it in that Monday morning, but not Adam. He proudly placed their castle in the library with all the others and prepared to present it to the class.

> *When it finally came time to present, needless to say Ruth did the majority of the talking and I did the majority of the watching. We took center stage and he did his thing. "See this sweet cup in the middle? Well, that's the king's quarters. And see this courtyard, that's where the knights joust and where they have competitions. This moat is the biggest one around so no one can cross," and on and on he went with the sales pitch of the year. It was amazing to me that something so simple and hastily assembled could be described in such a way that it might have been an actual scale model from the history museum. Yeah, to some it was a shabby middle school project thrown together with cups, cardboard and Elmer's glue, served up by someone who could really shoot the bull. To Adam it was a self-built masterpiece, and he was the master storyteller.*

* * *

Don't think, however, Adam and DJ didn't have their moments. They were great friends, but even the closest of friendships will occasionally go awry, and one winter day, sometime during middle school, this one did. School had been called off. DJ decided to make the short walk to Adam's house. When he arrived they started playing video games, listening to music, and horsing around. Charlene called around noon time to remind Adam that he had to snow blow the driveway and shovel off the steps before she got home from work. Adam managed to convince DJ to help him, so after lunch they bundled up and headed outside, Adam on the snow blower and DJ on the shovel.

> *Ruth's house had two driveways, one on each side. After we finished the one on the left, we moved to the one on the right. Adam was getting tired or bored and decided to spice up the snow removal. I was shoveling around the garage with my back turned to him when all of a sudden a wave of heavy, wet snow started hitting my back. It was so strong it actually knocked me down. I tried to get back up but it was difficult, because the power-assisted snow was already piling up around me. He had re-positioned the snow blower so that instead of blowing onto the lawn it was all being blown onto me. At first I was scared by what was happening but quickly went on defense and ran at Adam. He was laughing hysterically, like he had just pulled off the prank of the century. I managed to tackle him and tried to hit him with the shovel. What started out as a "funny" incident quickly turned into a fight. Because I tried to hit him with the shovel, Adam tackled me into the snow bank. He was yelling at me and telling me to take a joke. I tried to buck him off and fight my way out of his whitewash when all of a sudden, WHACK! The little shit had hit me in the back with the shovel. I dropped to the ground but managed to get back up and run through the open garage toward the house. I knew Adam wouldn't come after me and leave the snow blower running, and I'd already figured out how to get even, so I kept going with Adam screaming, "DON'T GO INSIDE SOAKING WET! MY MOM JUST GOT NEW CARPETS! DON'T YOU DARE GO INSIDE!"*

But into the house DJ went, soaking wet, jacket dripping, and boots leaving a trail of snow and dirty slush. Up the stairs he flew to Adam's room. He could still hear Adam screaming but he'd had to go back and shut off the snow blower. DJ looked quickly for anything important he could grab and saw the thing which Adam cherished above all else—his PlayStation memory card. By the time Adam had come inside, thrown off his jacket and boots, and raced upstairs to his room, he found DJ standing in front of an open window holding the memory card.

> *I knew in the back of my mind I was never going to toss it. I just wanted Adam to know that I was done playing and that he had messed with the wrong guy. My thoughts never made it to words, though, because before I could even say "truce," Adam tackled me into the wall near his window. I got up to fight back and he just kept yelling "I TOLD YOU NOT TO GO INSIDE! MY MOM IS GOING TO BE SO MAD! OUR NEW CARPETS ARE RUINED!" He then grabbed the cable that ran along the baseboard over and around the door into his bedroom, yanked it down, and with a crazed look in his eyes, told me to drop the memory card or he was going to choke me. I refused to listen and said I was going to throw it out the window. He then wrapped the cord around my neck and tried to make me pass out. Needless to say, I was terrified and started yelling for him to stop. In a matter of seconds, I dropped the memory card and he let go of the cord. He climbed off me and shut the window.*

DJ was pretty traumatized for a few minutes, not quite believing what had just happened. He thought about going home, but within two minutes of one of the scariest altercations of his life, Adam started laughing and jokingly kicked him in the ass and said, "Go clean up the water on the steps. My mom's going to be home soon. I'll go put away the snow blower." And just like that, the fight was resolved. No grudge, no peer mediation, no "talking things out." Adam was over what DJ had done and DJ was over what Adam had done: overreaction in the heat and cold of the moments. DJ went to clean up the footprints and water he had tracked into the house and Adam finished up the chores they had started together.

We were in the kitchen eating when Charlene got home. She thanked us for taking care of the snow.

* * *

The thing is, though, if you ever thought you had Adam figured out, you were wrong. One night during senior year, DJ was going to pick him up from Shaw's where Adam worked. Since they lived in easy walking distance of each other, many days they'd carpool to work, and this particular time DJ went to pick up Adam. It was probably 8:30 or 9:00pm and he'd been sitting out in the Shaw's parking lot for five or ten minutes waiting. DJ was one of the few kids in their group who didn't have a cell phone yet. He decided to go into the store to make sure Adam was still there. He walked in and looked around but Adam wasn't in the produce department where he usually worked. Instead DJ found him closing up the flower shop. Adam looked up and said, "Hey, man, sorry about running late. Misty didn't show up and the manager made me cover for her." He said he'd hurry up and be done in a few. DJ started back to his car to wait, but Adam insisted he just stay there while he finished.

When Adam had to go into the flower shop's back room he told DJ to come with him. Adam showed him the hose and power washer that he had to use to clean miscellaneous items: flower pots, holders, vases, anything that needed to be cleaned of soil or debris before it was put back on the front shelves or in the display refrigerator. There was a long metal bench, covered in dust, dirt, soil and plant trimmings. Ruth took the hose and just started spraying down everything in sight. It was obvious he was rushing to finish the job so they could leave, but it wasn't like they were in a big hurry. Still, Adam "cleaning up" that back room was one of the funniest things DJ had ever seen him do. He soaked every square inch of wall, using the hose as an all-in-one mop/broom/soap/rag/towel and just let it fly. Instead of wiping down the counters or sweeping up the floor, Ruth went ahead and treated the room like it was waterproof. There was water dripping from the counters, pots, vases, knives, trowels, shelves, light fixtures, outlets, you name it. Oh, it was clean, but *everything* was soaked. DJ stood there staring in disbelief. No way was he supposed to do that—*no way.*

"Dude!" I said when he finally turned the sprayer off, "what were you thinkin'?" He looked over at me and started to laugh. "Maybe she should have showed up for work today." I can only imagine what the person who went into the store the next morning thought when they first walked into that room. I can guarantee you this, Ruth had a convincing story for them—the kid just had a way with words.

* * *

Summer 2004 was am awkward time in DJ's life. During his freshman year of high school he had moved from his childhood home into a new house with his new step family. Thankfully, this new house was only a short walk from Adam's and throughout the four years in high school it was easy for him to escape the craziness of unfamiliar surroundings and new siblings by going to Adam's.

Being a stubborn teenager DJ never really accepted this move. His parents had recently divorced and his mom moved the family into this new house that never really felt like "home." The people living in the house quickly went from being "family friends" to family members. The whole ordeal was hard on DJ but the one thing he was grateful for was the location of this new house—it was close to Ruth's house. This turned out to be particularly important during the summer of 2004.

DJ, along with most of his friends, was excited to be getting ready for college in the fall, and he decided that working a lot was a good way to *not* be home a lot. He had turned eighteen in May and Market Basket, or "the Bucket" as the low level employees called it, offered him a full time position. His parents encouraged him to take on the forty-hours a week and learn responsibility—and get a good head start on saving money for college. In the end what was one of the toughest jobs he'd ever had also turned out to be one of the best summers of his life.

DJ began his new job right after graduation. A typical work week was Monday through Thursday, 7am to 4pm, with a mandatory one-hour lunch, plus either Saturday or Sunday. Some days his friends didn't even go to bed much before 7am, but if he wanted to go to college, keep his car running, and be out of the house, work was a necessary evil. On an average day he might spend the morning stocking the pasta aisle. So by twelve noon every day when the grocery department would break for lunch he'd be so done with hundreds of cellophane bags of spaghetti (regular, thin, and angel hair), rotini, shells (large and small), macaroni, ziti (regular and tri-colored)—yeah, you get it. Anyway, that was where Adam came in.

Most of DJ's co-workers were considerably older than he, so he wasn't really interested in sitting around in the break room listening to an hour's worth of complaints about the latest new rule from management or, even worse, stories about headaches and back spasms and sore joints. So what did he do? He drove over to Adam's house, two, maybe three times a week, just to hang out for the hour. He didn't even have to call to make sure it was okay to come by, it just was. Sometimes Adam would have a frozen entrée ready, or DJ'd pick up fast food on his way over. Since Adam was usually home alone and just waking up, unless he had to work, what they would do was eat lunch, then play video games and talk. Sometimes they'd talk about DJ's problems, sometimes Adam's, but usually they just talked about girls, sports, music, TV, and movies.

> *For three months, this was our routine, a regular part of the work week, and the salvation of my summer—something that was just the two of us. I helped Ruth get his day started and he helped me get through the rest of my afternoon. Oh, we still had our core group of friends and nighttime get-togethers where we could always find trouble, but our noontime lunch visits were different. As corny as it sounds, we were getting closer without even realizing what we were doing.*

* * *

In early September DJ moved into his new dorm room at UNH, a built-up triple, which meant it had almost enough room for two but because of overpopulation, the school had swapped out a twin for a bunk bed and told the students to deal. Three beds, three desks, three kids and no one knew each other until move-in day. DJ had a really tough time adjusting. Fortunately a couple of days later Adam came to visit.

It was Monday, September 6, 2004. By then I had a Nextel phone like the rest of my friends. All you had to do was push the button on the side and it was like a modern walkie-talkie. The person's voice just rang through. It was like their voice was the ring tone. I remember Ruth's voice coming through while I was just starting my day. He showed up a few hours later, about the time my classes were done for the day. He wanted to see my new digs. I told him to pick me up and we'd go park his car off campus and walk back. He thought that was nonsense and insisted on parking right by my dorm in a "faculty only" lot, assuring me he wouldn't get a ticket.

The boys walked up to DJ's dorm room and they just picked up where they had left off the last time they'd seen each other. The story of their friendship continued . . . only the setting had changed. First order of business was *Madden*. Second order of business was the girls. Adam didn't ask about DJ's classes, roommates, or about the whole college move that had seriously changed his life. Nope, all he wanted was to be sure he was still the better lady's man, and kick DJ's ass in *Madden* again.

See, for years, no matter how close their friendship, DJ was Adam's whipping boy when it came to *Madden Football*. Adam took this game seriously. There were out and out battles between Steven and him and Joey and him that were brutal, neither one speaking to the other during the entire hour-long contests. To most people video games are fun, enjoyable, and relaxing—but not *Madden*. Not to Adam, anyway. *Madden* has pride. *Madden* takes skill.

Even though he sucked at the game his whole life, DJ really enjoyed *Madden Football*. He liked the fact that all his friends played and that it really is one of the most *realistic* video games. Adam would beat him every time. The game had been around since they were in middle school and DJ might have beaten him two or three times—*maybe*—in a total of eight years. They'd start a game and be chit-chatting away, talking about some hot girl, and listening to Papa Roach or Linkin Park. Next thing you know it's 44 - 6 and Adam would tell him that he shouldn't have gone for it on 4th down in the 2nd quarter of the game. All he'd done was kick a couple field goals, to which Adam would remark, "field goals are for pussies."

> *I never really cared about losing in Madden, though. I knew I was the crash test dummy. Everybody loved to play with me because it was a sure W in the books. It didn't bother me—too much! I liked that it was something we all did, a link for our group, and something we all enjoyed. That day was no different. Ruth beat me up in Madden pretty bad and just like that, an afternoon had passed and it was time for him to leave. He gave me his signature hand shake as we walked back to his car and he made a big deal out of showing me he didn't have a parking ticket. He also told me to make sure I invited him to a party—once I found some friends!*

Chapter 4: Joey

I think it was in the third grade whent Adam and I met and we became best friends. Actually he was probably the closest thing to a brother I'd ever had. Adam was funny. Scratch that, he was . . . hilarious, hysterical, cool, confident, dependable, reliable, loud, smart, talkative, chill, athletic, happy, deep. He was so many things—at least to me he was. When we were bike-riding into Maine, he always led because he saw himself as the Maine expert since he'd lived in South Berwick once, when he was like six-years-old! He was forever competing for king of the Tire-Tanic during recess. 'Course you don't know the Tire-Tanic, but it was this thing made out of old tires roped together in the shape of a pyramid and you had to race to the top, and Adam almost always won. The kid was just the best at so many things.

We didn't have the same class together in the third grade but we became friends through other kids we both knew, and quickly found out we had a lot in common. One thing we shared was that we were both pretty smart when it came to sports, in particular professional sports knowledge. That discovery was made early on through trading sports cards amongst our group of friends. Looking back on it we were pretty crazy with all our trading. We'd memorize the stats and info on the backs of the cards, you know, stuff like college attended and awards won, and then try to barter with each other. I hate to admit it but Tim and I started calling Ruth "stat-man" because he was so good at memorizing the statistics and bios and then trading with people to his advantage. "Six-foot-two, two hundred fifteen pounds, throws left, attended Brigham Young University, born Jon Steven on October 11, 1961, in Salt Lake City, and was drafted in the first round, and first overall" got him a Steve Young card. And "Six-foot-two, two hundred pounds, born October 13, 1962, in Crawford, MS, attended Mississippi Valley State University, and was drafted in the first round, 16th overall, in 1985 by the 49ers" got him a Jerry Rice card. But "left-hand, left-field, six-foot-one, one hundred eighty-five pounds, Arizona State, first-round draft by the Pirates in the amateur draft" garnered him Barry Bonds! Not a whole lot of people can do that. Certainly not a whole lot of kids!

I'm tellin' ya, Ruth was so smart, which got lost on some of our teachers—I think because of all the craziness that goes along with kids and school, and our crowd in particular. But he was ridiculously smart. Whether we were playing Pee-Wee football, Madden, Tire-Tanic, competing with stats on his favorite NFL team, the San Francisco 49ers, or trading baseball cards, Ruth played to win—and mostly he did!

* * *

Adam and Joey didn't actually have a class together until eighth grade. Mrs. Dunlap and Mrs. Rogers. They became closer and more friendly throughout fifth, sixth, and seventh grades because they spent so much time together at school, particularly in sports, but their friendship really grew a lot in eighth grade. That year, the Somersworth Middle School football team went undefeated and won the middle school championship. Joey was the quarterback, Adam was the tight end, and Steven was the wide receiver. Joey had made a big pass completion to Adam in the championship game against Kennebunk, along with a touchdown pass to Steven. The pride he felt, getting to take the trophy home and have his mom and step-dad taking pictures with Tim, Steve, and Adam, was unbelievable. What a day!

By then, though, the bunch of them weren't just close in sports. Aside from finally having some classes together, the whole eighth grade got to take a field trip to a space camp in Canada that year. And did they have some times on that trip. It included an over-night at a hotel, and after chasing the girls around for a while, being ridiculously devious, they settled into their room for a long, crazy night. Joey, Adam, Tim, and Bodin, or maybe it was Austin, stayed up rather than going to bed, just doing dumb shit. They broke both headboards from wrestling on the beds, somehow flooded the bathroom, and knocked over the TV during another wrestling match. They threw water over the divider into the next room where Jared was staying; they'd already covered him in shaving cream and beaten him under a blanket earlier in the night. They made prank calls from their room phone, before they dropped and broke it. They tried to sneak out, but were re-directed back to their rooms by security. It's a miracle they didn't get the whole class thrown out of the hotel.

> *The memory which sticks out the most about that night, though, is Ruth. When we finally got back to our room and were maybe going to go to bed he got up, covered in the bed sheets, and paraded around the room repeating, "I'm Batman, I'm Batman, I'm Batman." Honestly, we didn't do any type of drugs at this point so when I think about it now, it's even more hilarious! He ended up getting into the adjoining room through the divider and doing his Batman bit in there, too. The kid was always good for laughs. He was forever wanting to make his friends happy, and being funny just seemed to come naturally to him. That's probably partly because he was a goofy motherfucker, and partly because he was truly good at it. Maybe he even had a career in comedy in his future.*

* * *

The summer between eighth grade and freshman year Adam and Joey spent a lot of time together, mostly doing stuff like riding bikes, going to the mall, the movies, and the beach. That was also the time, however, when they started sneaking into Joey's mother's liquor cabinet to steal her booze. He and Adam got banged up pretty good a few times early on. Probably because it was so new and so "bad," they really liked it. And they quickly discovered it was fun being drunk and stupid—too fun. They started stealing booze regularly. Joey's mother soon picked up on it, but he would just deny it every time and nothing would happen. Eventually they started replacing the booze they took with water. He wasn't sure if she didn't know or didn't want to know, but he was *pretty* sure . . .

> *There's one thing I'm certain my mother didn't know, because I've never told anybody: we started stealing her car. No licenses, obviously, yet. We'd go for rides when she was out with friends or whatever. Austin and Steve were often a part of these idiotic rides—some of which would be after we stole booze. One night I almost crashed while Austin, Ruth, and I were out on a drunken, underage, completely illegal joyride. We were all shit-faced, but for some reason it was funny—not dangerous. When we got back to my house, Ruth tackled Austin in my bathroom, putting a hole in the wall. We then walked from my house to a rock-a-thon at the middle school, a school-sponsored event. I was so drunk that one of our friends called her dad and had him bring me home. The getting home part I still don't remember to this day.*

As stupid as the whole night was, they all laughed about it the next day. Some good ol' fashioned fun. That was just one story of the many that could be told. Joey often wondered about him and Adam not having their fathers around, and if they would have done a lot of those crazy, dumb-ass things had they feared the consequences of a man coming down on them.

Joey figures he and Adam became so close because they were so much alike. They both acted similarly in social situations—loud, bordering on obnoxious at times, or maybe even over the border sometimes, and usually with an opinion to offer. Neither of them was ever afraid to speak their mind. They were both smart but also easily distracted. They were both very interested in girls, sports, movies, comedy, video games, being daring, and simply having *fun*. And maybe most importantly, they both were raised without their fathers present. Joey is certain that factored heavily into the way they grew up and, in particular, the way they lived their teenage lives.

> *I was talking with Steve about this very thing not long ago and we both feel like the lack of fathers had a huge impact on Ruth and me. There was no strong disciplinary figure in our lives, a stern, male voice to remind us about the consequences of our decisions, someone who could maybe speak from personal experience. Which could in turn have helped us avoid mistakes, or at least maybe helped us make fewer of them. It was no secret to anyone who knew Ruth and me in high school that along with being involved in athletics, we were also heavily involved in stuff we shouldn't have been. Our houses were places where people could go to do those things they couldn't do at their own houses. Yeah . . .*

* * *

Joey still remembers the first time he and Adam smoked pot. They were walking around Joey's neighborhood one night, drunk, after stealing booze from his house. It was maybe a couple weeks before the start of freshman year of high school. A car pulled up beside them. Several cute, older girls popped their heads out of the windows.

> *They invited us into the car and in we climbed. We were some excited to be with older girls and were having a good time just driving around with them, when they pulled out a pipe. I had never seen anything like it before, and had definitely never seen anyone smoke pot, but I think Adam had. Anyway, the pipe eventually made its way around to us and we were encouraged to give it a shot. Things only escalated from there.*

Once school started in the fall Adam and Joey were together a lot, mostly because of football, but they did drift apart some later in the year when Joey played basketball and baseball and Adam didn't. They still had good times together, but didn't hang out as much as during the summer and fall. With the end of the year, though, it was back to being best friends: always together and usually doing something illegal, mixed in with their other hobbies of video games, movies, and music.

By the time sophomore year was under way they had started smoking herb together pretty much every day. Some of their friends had begun getting cars by that time, which made getting drunk and smoking much easier. And, yeah, the escalation of weed was very relevant to Adam's story, and also to their relationship. Simply put, they believed marijuana did similar things for both of them.

> *With very high-strung personalities, smoking helped us in certain aspects of our lives. It helped to alleviate the daily struggles of classes, grades, parents—pretty much the stress of teenage life. There were ways smoking helped in social situations, too. Some may call this ridiculous but I've seen it and I've lived it. Many very real, very strong friendships were grown through hanging out in groups—often smoking weed. Football team nights in particular involved team bonding, and smoking was always a part of it. Like the time in our junior year when my mom and step-dad took the both of us on a Caribbean cruise. We got our groove on in the nightclub. Snuck in, of course. Played hoops on the top deck basketball courts, and shared deep thoughts during great convos while smoking Jamaica's finest on the balcony of our crazy room.*

Joey and Adam would often smoke and talk about personal stuff when they were high—and they were high a lot. They talked about living together on the west coast somewhere after graduating high school. Since they were both heavy into sports and Adam liked being funny, they would often talk about how they could make a hit TV show about sports and comedy. In fact they actually made some pretty crazy videos in Adam's garage. Sometimes, though, they'd just listen to music, watch movies, and play video games—and of course, get high.

> *If I'm going to be totally honest, though, I also have to admit there were negatives associated with our habit as well. Looking back on it, we and all of our other friends*

were absolutely abusing marijuana. Smoking way too much, smoking in public places, in cars, while driving, before school, after school, even before games and practices. It was pretty much the one constant within our circle of friends. If you were one of us, you smoked weed. And if you didn't smoke weed . . . well . . . you just weren't. Still, I can't help but wonder if the biggest problem with us smoking so much pot was the other stuff it eventually led to: shoplifting, hard partying, drinking and driving. Getting away with all of that stuff only contributed to the mindset that we were untouchable, invincible.

Chapter 5: Tim

Adam and I were best friends, though my earliest memories of him are a mixed bag. He could be a complete asshole one minute and your blood brother the next. Our relationship moved between wanting to punch him in the face to wanting to hug him. He was one of those kids who could be making fun of somebody at lunch and then do some random act of kindness for them a couple of hours later. Oh yeah, we were best friends but a lot of the time I loved to hate him.

I remember this one time, I think it was the summer between sixth and seventh grade, before we really got to know each other and became close friends. We spent a lot of time on our bikes during school vacations and that summer was no exception. This particular day we headed off to South Berwick, Maine. Ruth always led the way when we rode into Maine since he had lived there as a young kid. I think he felt like that gave him some kind of rights to being the leader. I'm sure what he remembered as a four or five-year-old was very valuable to his sense of direction and leadership!

Anyway, we ended up at the Little League field in South Berwick where we played home run derby for what seemed like about eight hours, but was probably more like two. It was one of those days where Ruth was just bugging the crap out of me. He could do that at times—and he was damn good at it. Just nitpicking, ya know? Poking fun at how I rode my bike and how I swung the bat or missed the ball or how much better he was. Just annoying kid stuff, but he was really getting on my nerves.

Then it happened, probably the maddest I have ever been at Ruth. He mumbled something under his breath to me as we were all going around the field picking up balls. "What did you say, Ruth?" I said to him, "I can't hear you." He looked up at me and in a loud, slow, condescending voice replied, "I said at least I don't have a nigger for a dad . . ." In that instant, I wanted to do two things. First, I wanted to run over and rip the kid's head off. Who does he think he is? I don't even really like him all that much and now he's going to insult me over the one thing in my childhood, besides my weight, that I am sensitive about. I don't remember what I said to him next, but I remember what I did—I started swinging. All of a sudden Joey was there and somehow he managed to get us both settled down. How, I have no freakin' idea.

It's weird that I can't remember how we got over the whole thing, but we did. In a way that kind of paints a small but pretty accurate picture of Ruth. He would say something stupid one moment, totally pissing somebody off, and the next you're at his house playing video games after a long day of bike riding, or football practice, or home run derby. Something about Adam drew us all to him, even if we didn't always like him or want to admit that we did. Remember I said before that sometimes we loved to hate him? Maybe it was more like sometimes we hated to love him.

* * *

Basically Adam was just a hard kid to figure out, more like impossible to figure out. When he was in one of his "philosophical" moods, he could talk about the most sophisticated things, like life after death, or God. When he wanted to be a dick, like with Tim's weight and his stepfather, he could be a major-league asshole. But when he was feeling funny he could be hilarious, like with the stunts he used to pull on Jared or Mr. Ready.

I'll never forget the field trip we took to Montreal for space camp in the spring of eighth grade. By that point in our lives we had begun to develop a sort of group persona or personality led by, you guessed it, Ruth. I probably should say it was "dominated by" Ruth. Maybe it was more of a reputation than a personality. Most everybody knew who was in our group and that if you saw one or two, the others were nearby. We weren't really "bad," but then we weren't really "good" either. Let's just say we liked to have fun, and our idea of "fun" wasn't always other people's idea of fun.

The teachers who had organized the trip, Mrs. Rogers and Ms. Dunlap, had stressed to the entire eighth grade that they were the first class to take such a trip. One of the biggest reasons the administration had allowed it was because their class, as a whole, had always shown excellent behavior. Either they were using reverse psychology or they missed factoring Adam and company into their calculations for behavior. That small group had a way of really skewing the average.

The number one thing drummed into us on the way up was being quiet and respectful when going from the United States into Canada. When we arrived at the Canadian border, a couple of agents came onto the bus. They asked if anyone was carrying over $500 in gifts or merchandise. Everybody said no. The guys looked around for maybe five minutes and then turned to leave the bus. As they were about to take their last step off Ruth yelled, "Hasta luego!" Everyone froze in disbelief. Did he really just do that? Did he really just yell something in Spanish to French Canadian border guards? Was he really being his typical smart-ass self when all the teachers were demanding excellent behavior and respect? But that was Ruth—flair for the dramatic.

Nothing too serious came from his outburst other than he got a first class seat right next to Ms. Dunlap. "Right here beside me, Mr. Routhier, until we get to Montreal—in about four hours!" For the kids, that was more than enough punishment all by itself. Everyone laughed and told the story for years. It was one of those Ruth moments that has never been forgotten. And, of course, within about a half-hour or so, Adam and Ms. Dunlap were back to normal talking and laughing, and within an hour he was out of punishment and sent back with us to talk about his latest stunt. That was Ruth, slick and silver-tongued like no other. That kid could convince a teacher to change an F to a D and make it feel like he was doing them the favor!

Of course that wasn't the only funny thing that happened on the trip. It was getting late when they finally got to the hotel and into their rooms. The first thing they discovered was that each room had sliders that opened onto a balcony. What better place could there be to holler to people down on the street—and in a foreign country no less! It also didn't take them long to figure out what section of the city they were in after seeing some of the people they were yelling to and the signs for this "Adult Club" and that "Adult Theater." For a few minutes they had a blast. Thankfully it didn't take the teachers long to figure things out and get them all moved to another section of the hotel. But not before providing Adam all kinds of clowning around material for the rest of the trip.

* * *

It was freshman year that we all started to smoke pot. I don't know who was first, but probably Evan because of his older brother. I was always against it and looked down on them at first for doing it. Within a few weeks, though, I caved. I guess fitting in was more important than the risk to our sports teams. If we weren't at Evan's house on early release days, we were at Joey's, smoking till the parents came home. And if we weren't at either of those places, we were in Ruth's bedroom. More typically we were at all of the above. We'd smoke at Joey's and/or Evan's after school, and then in Ruth's closet at night, and more often than not, we'd just end up sleeping over. There were times we'd lock ourselves in Ruth's room for hours. Every time Charlene yelled up to us, Ruth would yell back his famous line of, "Charlene, go to bed!" We laughed and laughed, as she acted like she cared, but in the long run I think it was easier for her to know where we were and to not know what was going on.

Charlene was the nicest lady, would do anything for us, probably too much, and I know we took great advantage of that. I remember on occasion wondering why she let us get away with so much. Now as I look back with more than ten years of hindsight and clarity, I can't help but wonder if it was out of guilt. She allowed Ruth to do pretty much anything he wanted with his friends, and I mean anything. Did she feel guilty that Ruth didn't have his father in his life, or that she'd had other troubles when he was young and wanted to somehow make up for it? I think maybe a little bit. But now I'm more inclined to believe she overindulged him—and the rest of us—because if we were in her house, at least she knew that by some definitions we were safe. At the very least, we weren't out driving around and hurting or injuring anyone—other than our own brain cells.

One night in particular was a standout. It was New Year's Eve during either our freshmen or sophomore year. Austin, Joey, Ruth and I were all in Ruth's room playing video games and what not. We would periodically crawl into his closet, which we had christened the "Cudaberry Clizo." It totally sounds like something four stoners would name their dope den. Anyway, we piled in the closet after we'd been doing stupid things all night: rough housing, throwing one another around, taking air duster hits from the can and spinning one another around until we fell over—very stupid things, now that I look back. Whatever, it was about eleven o'clock when the four of us piled into the closet. We were in there for what seemed like fifteen to twenty minutes. When the roaches were done burning our lips and fingertips, we started talking and drawing on the closet walls. When we finally opened the door, we all fell out, literally rolling out into Ruth's room. On the TV we noticed there was already a celebration going on so I looked at the clock. It was

12:33! We all looked at one another with faked surprise that we'd been in there that long—then we started laughing hysterically at the fact that we had totally missed all the festivities. It was dumb, illegal, and dangerous, but in some ways it was the best New Year's Eve of my life, which by now sounds kind of messed up to me. It wasn't the best for what we did, that's for sure, but for who I was with it was awesome.

Chapter 6: Jake

Jake lived in Rollinsford so he never even met Adam until, like all Rollinsford kids, he went to Somersworth Middle School in the seventh grade. Rollinsford is a very small town, one of the easternmost points in the southern part of New Hampshire, separated from South Berwick, Maine by the Salmon Falls River, from Somersworth, New Hampshire by a railroad track, a golf course, and a shopping plaza—in that order, and from Dover, New Hampshire by a long stretch of commercial property with Wentworth Douglas Hospital on one end and Dover Bowl on the other. Rollinsford was less than twenty percent the size of Somersworth. In general, Rollinsford kids weren't discriminated against, but sometimes they had to work to find their place. If you happened to be an outstanding athlete or musician, or exceedingly smart, that helped. If you were just an average kid, well, acceptance might be a bit more elusive. Jake was one of those more average kids.

> *I didn't know Adam much in middle school, partly because we weren't in the same home room and partly because it took the Somersworth kids a while to warm up to us anyway. In fact, some kids were just plain assholes to us. As small as it is, Somersworth is way bigger than Rollinsford, so they all thought we were just a bunch of small town hicks. Of course it didn't help my initial reputation that when Sarah Ellsworth asked me out my first week of seventh grade, I stupidly said no. She was probably the hottest girl in the whole school and I soon found out that the Somersworth guys figured I must be an idiot . . . or a wuss!*

Though Jake didn't really know Adam in middle school, he did know a few things about him. He knew he was popular, funny, and had a very distinguished laugh. He also knew Adam had a close-knit group of friends he wanted to be part of. He can remember thinking, *I don't want to be a Rollinsford kid, I want to be a middle school kid. I want to hang out with Steven and Austin, and DJ and Joey. I want to be cool like Tim and Adam.*

There's one other thing Jake remembers about Adam and middle school, which is that he royally pissed Adam off during their eighth grade trip to Canobie Lake Park. Jake's grandfather had just passed away and his friend Kendra was basically taking him on as a charity case for the day. It was a warm, sunny afternoon and they walked side-by-side for most of it. They did the bumper cars, the Canobie Corkscrew, and Pirata. She got him to try to win a stuffed animal at a ring-toss booth. Jake sucked at that stuff, though, so it didn't happen. Kendra even got him to go on the ancient Yankee Cannonball, a classic wooden rollercoaster. Jake was "freakin' petrified of rollercoasters!"

> *Then Kendra and I headed off to the food places and ate everything in sight. We started with pizza, fried dough, and French fries with cheese. Then we moved on to cotton candy and those super frozen ice cream dots. Come to find out I had been unknowingly pissing Adam off the whole day. I didn't know he and Kendra were "dating," and he was jealous that she spent the day with me. After that I figured I'd totally blown any chance of being friends with him. I was definitely not trying to steal his girlfriend.*

* * *

After two pretty difficult years in middle school, Jake was ready for high school, but he was pretty scared, too. He definitely wanted to be done with middle school but he wasn't at all sure he wanted to go to high school. What he was sure about, though, was that he really wanted to be friends with Adam's crew, and Adam in particular.

> *By the time I started high school, I was determined to break into Adam's group. My home life got weird after my parents divorced and my older brother had established*

> *a . . . less than great reputation at Somersworth High, so I was already worried. Also, I was a fairly small guy and I didn't want to be "pick on" fodder in high school. I just wanted to be a normal kid. Not "a Rollinsford kid." Not "a dorky kid." Not "the smart kid." I just wanted to be a kid. I wanted friends who accepted me as one of them, not as a butt for their teasing or their jokes, and who didn't make me feel like they were doing me a favor by letting me hang around with them. And somehow it happened, though I have to tell you I'm not at all sure how.*

The biggest obstacle was that Adam and his crowd were all on the football team. Jake was so *not* a jock. They were all bulked up and strong. He was the stereotypical ninety-pound weakling: skinny, twig-size fingers attached to pencil-thick arms, not a muscle to be found unless you counted his mouth. They were all tall, dark, and handsome. Jake was . . . not! But it still happened.

Jake still remembers walking through the halls of Somersworth High alongside Austin during their first days as freshmen. He hesitated but finally mustered up the courage to ask Austin if he could sit with his and Adam's friends at lunch. Austin said he'd ask Adam and the other guys if it was okay.

> *After school that day Austin messaged me on AIM and said it was cool if I sat with them. I always wondered if Austin took up my cause because he was almost as small as I was and that my presence raised his stature a little.*
>
> *Oh well, they probably could have given two shits if I sat with them or not, but I was so goddamn excited to finally be a part of a group of friends, especially one that I had admired for over two years—but always from afar.*

* * *

Jake will never forget the first time he and Adam made definite plans to hang out. It was a Friday and he was going to spend the night and most of the next day at Adam's house. It would be just the two of them and Jake was so excited he could hardly wait. As soon as he got home from school, Jake messaged BOMB266416, Adam's AIM screen name, and asked him what he wanted to do that night. Adam mentioned maybe watching some movies, so Jake started going through his stack of DVDs. He couldn't decide which ones to bring so he tossed all of them in a duffel bag and brought them with him.

> *Turned out that Adam didn't like anything I brought and so his cousin, "Fruity Pebbles" (don't ask me how he got that nickname), brought us to Walmart and Adam bought a movie. I couldn't have cared less what we did or what we watched. Adam had invited me to hang out with him and sleep over. I practically worshipped the kid and the thought of spending an entire evening and overnight with him was unbelievable!*

Jake doesn't exactly remember everything from that first time he stayed over at Adam's house, but he does remember that between the trip to Walmart, watching movies, and eating all the chips and cookies they could scrounge, he had a blast. Maybe that's why everybody liked going to Adam's house—not only was he a good friend but he was a great host. Like besides all the junk food and soda you could eat, if you slept over you could just sleep right in his bed instead of on the floor. They spent hours talking, munching, and AIM-ing with everybody they could find online and finally, sometime after midnight, they fell asleep watching TV.

> *I have no idea what time it was when I woke up. As I slowly moved from la-la land to groggy to semi-consciousness, I realized a few things: the movie had ended and the damn bright blue of the empty TV screen was streaming right into my eyes, I wanted a drink of water, and I kind of needed to pee. Now understand that Ruth was a really "messy" sleeper. As I thought of getting up I became aware of two other things: there was an arm across my chest and a leg crisscrossed over mine and Adam was sound asleep. Screw the TV and the bathroom. I just lay there, staring straight up to avoid the piercing*

blueness, not moving a muscle, barely breathing lest I wake him, thinking . . . Yes! There is a god!

* * *

That was the first time Jake stayed over at Adam's house but it wasn't the last. He always wondered if Adam ever figured out what a crush he had on him. He never mentioned anything, never asked why he didn't have a girlfriend, and never gave him shit or made fun of him for not dating anyone. The topic just never came up. In fact, it never came up with any of the guys. Almost instantly, Jake felt right at home in Adam's house. Meme and Charlene were usually around unless Meme was on a gambling trip to Foxwoods or Atlantic City, or visiting her sister in Rhode Island, or jetting off to Texas to see her son and his family. And they just sort of made Jake feel like part of the family.

If you were there around dinner time, Meme would feed you. Casseroles, tacos, sloppy joes with bread and butter—and you could help yourself to whatever you wanted in the fridge. It was always simple but delicious food. Like one night they had meatloaf with mashed potatoes and veggies. How could something so "regular" taste so good? Jake ate better at Adam's house than he did at his own.

Sometimes for breakfast in the morning they were on their own and they'd just have cereal with milk, orange juice, and toast. But every once in a while if Meme was home she'd make them pancakes or waffles. Adam's home became Jake's second home, a regular hangout, and they became close friends.

Of course I can't deny feeling one down to a lot of those guys, especially Adam. Neither can I deny that I had found a couple of Adam's weaknesses, and they were pretty easy to exploit. Like besides watching movies and just "hanging out," he also liked to smoke pot. Sometimes that was my in with him. I might message him during the day and say, "Hey, let's hang out tonight and watch a movie. I'll bring the weed." How could he say no to that? Usually he didn't. It's like I had this need to continually earn that "close friend" status.

One day Jake decided to impress Adam by driving one of his parents' extra cars over to his house—before he had a driver's license. Once or twice his mom had let him take her '97 Toyota Celica around the block of their quiet subdivision to practice driving a standard shift. This particular afternoon he called Adam and said he was going to quickly stop by while he was "practicing." He only lived a couple miles away and Jake thought he could get away with it, which he did. He literally pulled in Adam's driveway, knocked on the door, showed him he was driving the car and took off to go back home.

At some point not too much later Jake decided to risk a little more. On an early release day from school he told Adam he would teach him how to drive a standard, even though neither of them had their license yet. Well, word got out pretty quickly and before long Joey took his mom's Camry out and they ended up racing around Rollinsford in their parents' cars.

One thing's for sure, when Adam did something, he didn't mess around. It was all or nothing. Man, he scared the shit out of me that day. Oh, it was funny at first and we were laughing our asses off while I was trying to teach him how to drive a standard—the car bucking around, stalling, then bucking some more—but when he wanted to show off in front of Joey, no amount of yelling at him to "slow down" slowed him down. I dropped his ass off at home as soon as I could and though we did have a few more joyrides after that, I did all the driving. I loved Adam, I mean I really loved Adam . . . but I liked me pretty well, too.

Chapter 7: Andy

Andy and Adam became best friends when Andy moved back to Somersworth, partly because they lived pretty close to each other. Andy's family had moved to Massachusetts, but they were only gone for a few months. When they got back to Somersworth, they moved into a house just a couple of blocks away from Adam and come to find out Steven had saved his seat at school, so life was good. Most days Adam and Andy walked to school together and would meet up with Steve, Austin, and Joey once they arrived. Since they all played football together, at least one of them usually had a ball for passing or a quick pick-up game.

Football was by far our greatest bond. By middle school our team was looking pretty freakin' solid. Adam was tight end and linebacker, or sometimes safety. Steven was running back and linebacker, too. I can't quite remember what position Austin played. During the season if we weren't in class or sleeping or eating, we were playing football, either in a practice or a game.

On weekends and after school we still played. There was this place behind the neighbor's house we called Half Hill. We'd play pass or tackle football for hours. The place was pretty treacherous 'cause the bumps and holes were deceiving, but you got used to it. Our crowning achievement was our Pee Wee football team going undefeated in the sixth grade. It was the absolute best! I still have my jersey from that year somewhere. Go, Lions!

* * *

Football wasn't the only connection they had, though. Even before middle school started, video games were becoming the new pastime. Obsession is more like it.

The back room was where Ruth and I played video games. It was where you came into Ruth's house from the garage. One of our favorites was Resident Evil. *It was a survival horror game based on zombies and the corporation that controlled them. But the one we played even more than that was* Dynasty Warriors. *We loved that game. It was a hack 'n slash game based in old China. There were different warriors you could play as and then do battle in wars. The thing that made it so much fun was we could play together as a team battling these Chinese dudes. We could get new weapons, too, when we needed them. It was awesome.*

Maybe our most favorite, though, was Final Fantasy. *They have about fifteen games out. They're all a little different but have pretty good stories. Like* Dynasty Warriors, *you battle as a team with characters you meet along the story line. I can't even guess how many hours upon hours I spent playing that with Ruth when we were kids.*

High school brought a lot of changes for Andy and his friends. By the time football practice started freshman year, weed had become the new favorite pastime. The problem was, Andy wasn't really interested in pot. That's not to say he didn't do it—most kids will go along with their crowd, but he didn't really want to and he didn't enjoy it. As they began smoking more and more, Andy found himself hanging out with them less and less, though when he was with them, he usually caved and smoked.

I think it was my junior year when things got really bad. We were over at Ruth's in the garage smoking weed. I remember lying on the floor doing a cone—and I must have lost consciousness at some point. I don't remember how I got there but I obviously made it home because I can remember my mom asking me if I was okay. The next thing I remember is waking up in the hospital. Ruth and somebody else came to the hospital to see me. I also remember how pissed my mother was. She called our coaches and told them everything: "Not only was my son's phone destroyed, he could have died! This is what you people call 'Team Night'!" I remember a bunch of kids were suspended because of it and I think some were kicked off the team, too. I was pretty much ostracized after that.

That's the truth. Andy continued to play football with them the rest of that year, but basically they just stopped calling him for anything else. He didn't play his senior year.

Chapter 8: Mrs. Drew

The Drew brothers lived a couple doors away and Adam was at their house or they were at his much of the time. Mrs. Drew thought he was the cutest gosh-darned little thing, but what a handful. She couldn't help but wonder how his mother and grandmother managed to get through every day—and keep him alive! Oh, she loved him to pieces, from the day she met him, but talk about mischievous. The boy had more energy than a nuclear reactor, which often ended up causing trouble when everyone was in the house. It didn't take long for Mrs. Drew to realize that Adam could get himself into trouble even while he was sleeping. But always with that smile.

> *Oh my God, what a kid! Lucky me, as soon as Adam moved into the neighborhood with his sister and mother, he made friends with my sons. I remember one time, he couldn't have been more than five or six, Adam climbed up in a chair and then up onto my ironing board. Down it went: collapsed and broke. Fortunately he wasn't hurt, but the ironing board was history. Another time we evidently weren't answering his knocks fast enough and so he knocked louder . . . with a hammer! Twenty or so years later the small dents are still in our front door.*

Then there was the fire incident. Once the kids were a bit older Mrs. Drew's mother, who lived next door, would check up on the boys when they got home from school until Mrs. Drew or her husband got out of work. One day, Mrs. Drew's mother saw a fire coming from behind their lilac bushes. She rushed over and there was Josh, his older brother Chris, and Adam. They had started a small bonfire and Adam had thrown some of his toy dinosaurs into the flames. They didn't think anything was wrong with this. Later when Mrs. Drew got home, she assured the three of them that they were lucky it was her mother who had discovered them and put the fire out. If it had been reported to the fire department, they could have been charged with something. They didn't believe her, but it was spring time and the newspaper was full of stories about brush fires and kids getting in trouble. She cut out every article she could find, sat them down, and made each of them read every single one. They finally got the point—after several weeks of reading.

> *Adam certainly was a handful, but then I guess mine were too when I think about it. The saying is, it's a wonder kids live to grow up. I think maybe it should be. It's a wonder parents live to grow old.*

* * *

There were always a lot of kids around the Drew house, especially summers, or any time school was out, really. One reason was because they had a swimming pool. It was just a small one, twelve feet round and three feet high, but you did need a ladder to get in and it had a small pump. It was big enough for their age group and there were a couple of really hot summers while Mrs. Drew was still home with the kids and not working. She didn't have a car in those days so the pool got used a lot. Of course she had to be right there supervising constantly, because, with that whole crew in the water, sometimes things would get rough. She never knew who or what would get shoved, knocked, or broken. Could be a float, but it might also be toys, boys, or bones!

One time the whole bunch of them were in the pool. Along with the two Drew brothers there was Steven, DJ, Tim, Joey, and of course, Adam—all of them. There were a lot of horseflies around and they all hated the darn things. If a horsefly landed on one of them, that kid would cry out *horsefly!* and they'd all dunk under the water and come up splashing. They even started a club they called the Horseflies and used the shed in the back yard for a clubhouse.

> *There was a huge sandbox out back and they spent a lot of time in that with trucks and water when they were little. We also had a lot of trees at the very back of our yard, along with a couple of huge lilac bushes. Every once in a while I still find little Matchbox cars and*

marbles and such back there among the lilacs and poplars when I'm trimming and pruning.

Beyond the back of their yard there was a strip of woods before you got to the neighbors' open field. The kids built a lot of forts out there. One summer they worked every morning for days gathering up wood, hammers, nails, and saws and heading out to build. The boys did get permission from the neighbors, but they probably thought they'd build *a* fort, not two or three. They also used to set off rockets out in that field. Chris had an interest in rockets and bought new ones regularly. An adult always went along for the launch, usually Mrs. Drew. They'd get things set up, fire one off and then spend the next hour or so searching for it.

I don't think they ever caused a problem with the rockets but they did often roam beyond the trees and got themselves into trouble a couple of times. I well recall a broken window and sticks getting into the neighbor's pool. Both of those times an adult showed up at my door looking for the culprit. Of course they all denied it at first, but eventually a window had to be paid for. Funny, but I could always count on Adam to tell the truth—even if it took a while.

The boys also played a lot of wrestling games. As a little kid, Adam was the weakest of the gang and lost all of the time, but the others would let him win once a week or so to keep him wanting to play. Who knows why, but they gave him the name, "Ultimate Adam."

Besides the pool, another summer favorite was asking to sleep out overnight in tents. I only agreed to it a few times because I didn't really trust them to stay in the tent and not roam the neighborhood during the night. God only knows what might have gotten broken or ended up in somebody's pool under the cover of darkness.

After they got a second car, Mrs. Drew would brave a day trip with them once in a while. The beach was the worst! She only did that once because it was way too hard to keep track of them, even with *two* adults. The only time she knew where they all were was when she handed out quarters for the arcade. The beach trip was basically a parental nightmare. She eventually opted for places like Chucky Cheese, Hilltop Fun Center, or Jokers, because she could hand out tokens a few at a time, so they had to keep coming back for more. It was about the only way she could keep tabs on them.

Sometimes I still wonder how I survived those years . . . but more often . . . I wonder where they went . . . Chris, Josh, and Ultimate Adam.

Book Three

Mr. Mac and Colleagues

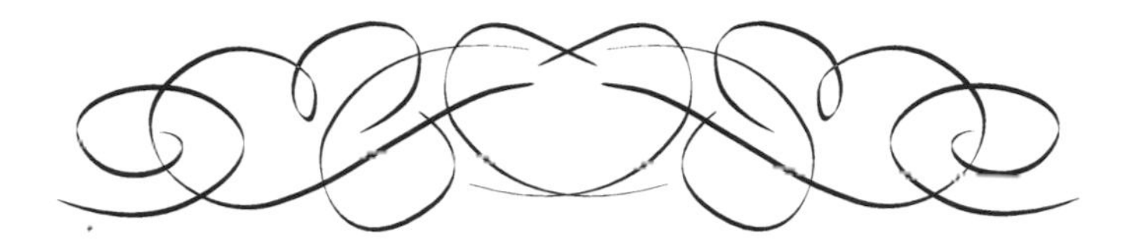

Chapter 1: Mr. Mac

Usually when I encounter someone who is full of the proverbial bluster and bravado—you know the kind I mean, the person who exudes close to too much confidence, but not quite, who typically enters every room mouth first—I tend to wonder what they're trying to cover up, where their insecurities and vulnerabilities are, what their *real* story is.

But not Adam. Not him and not his crew. I don't know, but maybe I was jealous of them, sort of. I mean, they were everything I wasn't as a kid: popular, confident, good looking, athletic. That's why I found it so weird that they warmed up to me so quickly. 'Course as odd as it may sound, maybe *they* were a little jealous of *me*. By that point in my life, I suspect they saw me as pretty successful. I'd been married for a long time, worked at a job I loved, drove decent cars, lived in a nice house, and owned two vacation homes. For whatever reason, during school hours they took me into their group for almost their entire four years at Somersworth High.

I was in my classroom by or slightly before 6:00 every morning that school was in session. I read and graded papers. I wrote lesson plans. I emailed parents, students, and colleagues. I posted grades. Every once in a while I'd even have to do the reading I had assigned for homework the day before (but don't tell anybody that!). I'd cut pictures of my students from the sports pages of our local newspaper and hang them up. I'd work non-stop for about an hour, but when 7:00 came, I grabbed my bagel and headed to the cafetorium for coffee. After that it was up to our hall, the place where Adam and company gathered before classes began. It was the second floor, outside the last science rooms, where we all pulled up some floor space, ate our breakfast, and kibitzed.

We had our morning breakfast group for the better part of four years. And if I had some parent conference or an IEP meeting or something and couldn't make it, I heard about it later in the day. Come to think of it, in a way we were a family even before I started hanging the banner in my classroom that said we were. And we were friends way before I had them in class: Adam, Tim, Jake, DJ, Steven, the lot of them. All these years later, I still see us sitting on the floor in that corner of the science wing every time I walk through it.

* * *

It was his senior year and I had Adam for two classes, three hours a day! Most days I loved to see him come through my door. He usually had his trademark smile, part happy grin and part sly smirk, and you couldn't quite tell on any given day which part was the most dominant—but you'd find out. He most often came in with his Adam swagger, too, a cross between confident and cocky, weighted slightly toward the latter. His normal dress consisted of pressed jeans, pressed polo shirt, the short sleeves of which were stretched to capacity with bulging biceps, and sneakers that looked like they'd just come out of the box. If one had checked, I suspect his socks and underwear had been ironed, too.

I never really understood why Adam liked me so much, though there was no doubt he did. I was a teacher. He did *not* want to be a student. He had been a good athlete most of his life. I was a jock wannabe. He could not contain his muscles. I could barely find mine. I expected students to be quiet and attentive in class, at least when I was talking. Adam could not keep his mouth shut, *especially* when I was talking. There was almost always a dialog or *trialog* running between him and his crew. I cannot tell you how many times a day I asked for quiet. Some days it made me crazy. But still he liked me, and, God only knows why, I liked him, too.

I finally learned that there was another side to Adam, a more sensitive and vulnerable side than the one he had on public display. Oh, there was the ever-popular, always-in-control, never-admit-a-mistake, never-let-your-guard-down Adam, to be sure. But there was also the I'm-not-so-sure-about-this, I-don't-understand-how-this-can-bother-me-so-much, why-do-I-hurt-so-bad side of Adam as well. It wasn't until my Intro to Philosophy class, that this other Adam began to make his appearance—not publicly but privately, in his writing and in our conversations.

* * *

"Mr. Mac, can I talk to you sometime—after school—like maybe today?" queried Adam.

"Of course. I'll be here." Ah, I supposed, he's finally figured out he is seriously falling behind. But that wasn't it at all.

Classes ended at 2:20 pm and it was just about 2:21 when he got to my room, a very different Adam Routhier, one without the swagger, without the air of confidence, without the impish grin and glint in his eyes. Even his biceps seemed to bulge a bit less that afternoon. Adam sat down across from my desk, just the two of us, and I said, "So what's on your mind?" I don't remember exactly what I expected but it was nothing like what I got. He began.

"Mr. Mac, I feel like such a loser."

My mouth stayed silent for a moment but my mind journeyed swiftly. Something wasn't adding up. Yes, the boy rarely got work in on time and it was even rarer that the quality equaled his ability. But dear God, forget the swagger and semi-cockiness, he exuded this sense of . . . *invulnerability*.

"Adam, I could have imagined all kinds of ways in which you might have begun this conversation but that was not one of them. Why on Earth would you feel like a loser?"

There were several seconds of increasingly awkward silence before the *in* came off, and I saw the *vulnerability* he had so successfully kept hidden. He looked me in the eye, almost, and replied, "Mr. Mac, all I do is smoke weed. Every day, two or three times most days. I smoke after school. I smoke when I get out of work. Sometimes I even smoke before school. My grades suck. I'm not sure I'm going to pass history. I'm not even sure I'm going to pass your English class. I've already lost one girlfriend and even though I work a lot, I can't ask anybody out because I can't afford to do anything. I can't hardly put gas in my car. Just about every penny I make goes to buy weed. It's possible I won't even graduate. Seriously, Mr. Mac, I feel like *such* a loser . . . and I don't know what to do about it. I'm just sort of . . . caught.

I sat there staring at this well-dressed, good looking, athletic, popular, bright young man, a guy seemingly about ready to graduate high school and take on the world, who's telling me he feels like a loser. "Adam," I finally offered, "if you truly feel that way, why don't you stop doing it?"

His answer made all the sense in the world to anyone who has ever been a teenager: “Because all my friends do it, and I want to be with my friends.”

* * *

Because my friends do it, and I want to be with my friends. I will never forget that statement or that day. I looked across my desk and just stared at him for several moments, rewinding and then fast forwarding through some of the times when my actions shamed me, when I knew I should do something else, when I felt like “such a loser,” and eventually I got it. I understood where he was, and at least in part how he got there. For most teenagers there is little in life as momentarily important as fitting in with their friends.

When I arrived back at the present, I knew I needed to try and help Adam in some way. He was clearly not there after all simply to make small talk—he wanted help. I looked at him a moment longer and said, “Adam, do you trust me?” “Of course,” he quickly responded, “You know I do.” “Do you love your mom?” I asked. “Absolutely,” came his reply. “I think we need to enlist Mom’s help with this. Think about what it would do to her to find out the day before graduation you were not going to graduate. How would that make her feel? How would it make *you* feel? I *know* she needs to be involved with your academic troubles and I believe she needs to be involved in your struggles with pot as well.”

He continued to meet my gaze, perhaps with just a touch of skepticism, but agreed to let me set up a meeting with the three of us. “The thing is, Adam, this has to come from you. I’m not going to tell her you have the drug problem. I can talk about all the school stuff but the drug problem has to come from you—because you have to want the help. I gave you my word that our conversation would be between the two of us and I’m going to keep my word—I’m going to give you that. I am not going to tell her, but I will provide the opportunity, with me here for support, for *you* to tell her.”

By the time I was done talking, his face had drifted down a bit. When he looked up again he seemed a bit tentative but willing to try and work out a plan with Mom that would make his life better and help him get back to a decent place, both academically and emotionally. When we finished making plans for our meeting, I said, "Is there anything else I can do for you?" He looked at me and replied, "I could really use a hug." "Kid, you can always have one of those," I said with a smile as we stood and wrapped our arms around each other. Even as we hugged, though, I couldn't help but wonder how much more there was about this boy that I didn't know.

* * *

The day following our after-school chat, Adam and his mom came in to talk. I had never met his mother and I remember feeling a bit sad that we had to meet under such strained conditions. I much prefer parent meetings when I can stick to all the good things about a student. I suspect she was also a bit sad or maybe embarrassed. She was pleasant but very reserved and very willing to let Adam and me do most of the talking.

I started by explaining some of the broader issues Adam and I had been discussing and then revealing my belief that nothing was likely to change unless we had her support and reinforcement. If Adam was going to graduate, something he claimed he absolutely wanted to do, he was going to need her to push him.

We talked about papers that needed to be written and homework assignments that needed to be completed. We talked about the number of hours he was working—clearly too many to keep up with his academic load. We talked about eating and sleeping habits and chores at home. We talked about socializing, both in school and out, and his increasingly desperate need to focus. Basically we talked about everything *except* what we really needed to talk about.

Finally we had exhausted all the symptomatic topics. We needed to talk about the real problem.

"So, Adam, we've gone over everything you need to make up to get current. We've talked about what you need to do, the changes you need to make so you can keep up with future assignments. Mom has said she will be a constant reminder and check in with you regularly. Is there anything else you can think of that would help you get through these struggles?" I queried.

"Uh, no, I don't think so," he responded.

Come on dude, don't do this to me—don't do this to yourself. "There's nothing else you can think of that needs to happen?"

"I, um . . . I think we've talked about everything."

No, please don't cave on this. Nothing will change. You told me you could do this. Please! "So there's nothing else you can think of that we need to talk about in order to give you the best shot at making things better for you?"

"Ah, I can't really think of anything—can you?"

Nooooooo! Don't do this to me, damn it! We agreed that this had to come from you in order for it to matter! I promised you that I was not going to bring it up. Come on, Adam—you have to do this. You have *to!* . . . "Nope, I guess not." And with that, we gave each other a hug. I gave Mom a hug and the meeting was over.

Adam pulled it together enough to pass the necessary courses and earn the required credits to graduate. But a few months later, I would confront that final response again. The decision to honor my word would haunt me for years.

Chapter 2: Mrs. Crockett

Some things in life, some people in life, are forgettable. For Sandy Crockett, his third grade teacher, Adam Routhier was not one of them. It was her first year as a classroom teacher at Maple Wood Elementary School. In some ways it was the year from Hell for Sandy. She had just recently filed for bankruptcy. Then she had to try and sell a lot of what she owned so she could move into a smaller place. It was a very difficult and trying period of life for her.

Then in September of 1994 Sandy found herself standing in front of a brand new classroom full of third graders. It was the first day of school and she remembers looking at them, seeing them looking at her, all ready to experience the "new teacher," and thinking, "Oh, my!" She introduced herself saying, "My name is Mrs. Crockett and I'm looking forward to being your teacher this year." It was Adam who initially broke the ice.

> *This cute, brown-haired boy right away asked me what my first name was. I went ahead and told them it was Sandy. So this same cute, little, brown-haired boy all of a sudden starts singing the Davy Crockett song, but substituting my name: San – dy – , San – dy Crockett. I was about to gently reprimand him but instead started laughing, along with the rest of the class. Both names had two syllables. He had the right tune. And it was pretty creative, particularly for a third grader!*

* * *

Of course as cute as Adam was with his dimpled chin, bright eyes, and incredible smile, he was also a handful—just "full to running over" with energy, which sometimes was hard to contain and frequently got him into trouble. Mrs. Crockett seated him front and center most of the year to help him focus better. Adam wasn't diagnosed with ADHD but he was definitely hyper-active and *very* hyper-distractible. He was also quite athletic and was especially fond of group games at recess. He loved gym class but had little use for music class, his now favorite TV tune notwithstanding. He was a pretty typical third-grade boy in most ways.

> *One of the things I remember most vividly about Adam actually happened when I was out of school with pneumonia. The day I returned after being out sick for several days in December, I was called into the principal's office. My first thought was, "Uh oh, what did I do wrong? I haven't even been here." Then she told me that during my absence Adam had been suspended for three days because he had tied a girl to a tree during recess—using her jump rope.*

There was a parent meeting over that incident right after Sandy returned to school. She could tell just from that short meeting with her that his mother had a difficult time handling him.

> *At times, so did I. You know, he was the only child I ever had suspended in all my years as a classroom teacher. But he was also the only student I ever had who serenaded me! You almost had to love him—and Lord knows I did.*

Chapter 3: Mrs. Rogers

The combination of Adam and any one of his friends could be, not exactly lethal but definitely not studious—even when it was supposed to be. Make no mistake, Adam was smart enough. He just didn't always apply his intelligence to academics. And if anyone else was involved, he almost never did. Like the time Mrs. Rogers and Ms. Dunlap took the kids on that field trip to the Science Center in Montreal.

> *It was the first time we had taken our class on the Montreal trip and, well, my chaperones and I thought we had everything under control. But not so much, as it turned out. It started when the French Canadian border guards finished inspecting our bus. As they were stepping off, Adam yelled out "hasta luego" to them. Graciously they pretended not to hear. Then we found out upon arrival that the hotel we picked was still under construction and the staff refused to speak to us in anything but French. Turned out, those matters were nothing because we also discovered, to our great embarrassment, that we were smack in the middle of Montreal's red light district. Adam and his crew told stories about that for weeks!*

Their original assigned rooms all had sliders to an outside balcony, and it was the kids who noticed the "ladies" walking down on the street below. Adam, Joey, and Steven were among the very first to display their excitement and ask to go outside! Thankfully they were able to move everybody to a different floor and in a different section of the hotel—overlooking the parking lot. Of course, much to the teachers' chagrin, they discovered that some "business" got conducted there as well. Fortunately, once they got moved and settled into new rooms, with boys at one end and girls at the other, most everyone was pretty well exhausted.

The day we left I overheard some of the boys—especially Adam—bragging about all the ruckus they'd caused in their rooms the night before. I probably should have punished him, or them, but I chose to believe that their damage estimate was a little exaggerated because even if we had missed it, I'm pretty sure the hotel would have found a way to charge us. If he just didn't have that darn smile!

A Foster's newspaper reporter came and interviewed the students and teachers when they got back to school so parents and people in Somersworth could see what they had done and how much they had learned. Even the teachers were pretty impressed to read back over all they had packed into the trip. Oh, they'd had to tweak the itinerary a little bit once or twice, but not much really.

And we were able to break up the long ride home with a stop at the Ben and Jerry's plant in Vermont. Ice cream can make almost anything better. In all honesty, Adam and company notwithstanding, it was a great trip—especially for the first year. How weird is it that I still remember him ordering cookie dough ice cream?

Chapter 4: Señor Becerra

Jose Becerra is a past-middle-age, soft-spoken, fairly low-key, *tranquilo* kind of guy. He keeps his emotions pretty much to himself and doesn't get too riled up—at least not visibly. Don't think, though, just because he may not show them, that he doesn't have feelings, because he definitely does. Things and people and students can, and often do, make him happy, irritate him, or ¡*hacerlo loco*! There are even those rare people and students who do all three. Such a student was Adam, particularly when he had Señor for Spanish IV his senior year.

> *Adam was one of the laziest, most unmotivated, habitually procrastinating students I ever had. Never do today what can be done tomorrow? Not even close. More like never do today what should have been done yesterday—or even the day before. Put it off, put it off, put it off, and pretend it's not hanging over your head. And then, when the semester is all but over, when your academic world is about to come crashing down, you're about to fail, and the failure will prevent you from having the minimum number of credits you need—then the guidance counselor shows up in my room to advocate for you. Then the principal happens to run into me in the hall to let me know that without my credit you won't have enough to graduate. Then your mother shows up to plead your case. That was my experience with Adam during the second semester of his senior year.*

Yes, every word you just read was the truth, but it wasn't the whole truth, and that's not referring to some of the other things Señor knew about him, some of the darker things going on in his life. What he means is that it was only a part of his story with Adam. The fact is he really liked Adam, even though in many ways—maybe in most ways—that made no sense at all.

When you get right down to it no one, no matter how much they can irritate and aggravate, is all bad, and Adam definitely had some good qualities. For instance, Adam sat in the front row during Spanish IV, and he always demonstrated considerable self-respect. His hair was clean every day and he dressed well. His clothes were neat and pressed—no dirty jeans or shirts with holes or threads hanging. He always looked "put together."

> *Another good quality about Adam was that he was always, virtually always, polite. He never made rude comments or told crude jokes or anything like that, so he rarely had to apologize or say, "I'm sorry." There was nothing to apologize for. And he never defaulted to "I don't know." If I asked him a question in class he would always at least attempt an answer. If he wasn't sure, he'd give it a shot. If he didn't exactly know how to pronounce something in Spanish, he'd try his best.*

In those days Señor had a colleague who was a very good dancer and he used to ask her to come in and teach his students the Merengue and the Salsa. There is nothing Adam wouldn't try. There was the sexy hip-twisting and two-step foot patterns of the Merengue, while trying to keep body movement from the waist down. And they tried the Salsa with its hand swings and bouncy steps and turns. Those were not easy for kids raised on American rock 'n roll fast dancing.

> *And I haven't gotten to the singing yet. There was nothing we did that Adam didn't put his best effort into, and I don't mean that silly little days-of-the-week song to the tune of "Frère Jacques" either. We did some pretty good stuff, like "Bidi Bidi Bom Bom" by Selena, "Eres Tu" by Luis Miguel, Celia Cruz's "Oye Como Va," and even Ricky Martin's "Livin' la Vida Loca." Honestly, if I could have graded him solely on effort in the classroom, Adam would have gotten straight A's, A pluses in fact.*

The problem was that grades included more than that—much more. There was homework and vocabulary and short papers and tests—all of which required studying. Students had to learn new tenses and moods and the corresponding endings. There were verbs to conjugate, singular, plural, and reflexive pronouns to master, and adjectives to which they were often attached. Students had substantial amounts of new material being regularly presented —most of which Adam regularly ignored.

So when early June came around, Señor became the target of last resort. All these years later he can still see Adam's mother sitting in his room tearfully pleading her son's case: "He is in such a bad way, just in a really bad place with difficult stuff tearing him apart. Can you please forgive him?" Truthfully, at the time it made him angry. Part of him really wanted to ask why she hadn't been here three or four months before—even one or two would have been a help. But he didn't, he just sat there trying not to show how upset he was, knowing that in all likelihood his fondness for the kid, not Mom's request, would win and he would cave.

I remember, too, bumping into Bob Fisher, my principal, in the hall and having him "let me know" that if I didn't cut Adam a break he would not have enough credits to graduate. I got the impression that he was being so blunt because he thought I'd be a hard ass with Adam's grades if he wasn't. That made me even angrier than the guidance counselor or his mother, frankly.

He thought about not doing it, about not giving in and keeping Adam's grades exactly what he had earned.

I'd already made up my mind, though, that Adam in person, in the flesh, was way more important than Adam on a report card. So I did what I had to do in order to live with myself. Basically I did grade him mostly on "effort in the classroom." I caved and cut him the break he needed to graduate with his class. If you could see the score sheet I've kept on him all these years, you would see just how much I caved. I didn't regret doing it. Less than three short months later I was thanking God I had done it. I think I even silently thanked Bob and Adam's mother for the nudge, whether I had needed it or not.

Chapter 5: Coach

It was a Monday, the first practice after a weekend game and Coach was pissed. At the last Team Night, which happened to be in Adam's garage, one of the players had gotten really messed up, and another player's cell phone had been totally destroyed and the parents of that kid, the one with the ruined phone, had been on the horn to Coach. "This is what's going on at your *Team* Nights!" the parent hissed as she described the rampant alcohol and drug use.

Coach hadn't wanted to upset the whole team before the game, but now that it was over he could lay them out—and he did! With the parents having blown open the whole weed thing, and the drinking, he finally had evidence he needed to do something. Even if the coaches had wanted to "look the other way," which they didn't, they couldn't, not if they wanted to salvage any shred of their substance abuse policy and protect the integrity of the program—not to mention the school's reputation. So they sent the JV packing and sat the varsity's butts down on the practice field and let them have it.

"What is wrong with you guys? Do you realize how far we can go this year? There is a lot of talent on this team—but it's obvious now that there is a lot of stupidity, too."

No response.

"A bunch of you were on the middle school team that won the championship your eighth grade year. We thought you wanted another championship before you graduated—were we wrong?"

No response.

"Is getting high important enough to you to blow everything you've worked for, most of you for the last four years?"

No response. Just a lot of looking down, around, and away.

"Talk to us, you guys—we absolutely have to deal with this. We can't just ignore it or pretend it didn't happen. We have to take our roles as coaches seriously even if you don't take your roles as players seriously."

"Coach, we *do* take being players seriously," someone finally said. "This really isn't that big a deal."

That's when Coach finally lost it. "Not a big deal?" he screamed. "What the hell are you talking about? Of course it's a big deal!" The yelling continued with, "Even if we ditch the discussion about what you're doing to your minds and bodies, you signed a friggin' contract *promising* to abide by the substance abuse policy—which is NO USE OF ILLEGAL SUBSTANCES! PERIOD! You gave us your *word.*"

Again, no response. Just more downcast eyes.

> *Maybe the biggest thing that really got to me was the fact that they knew it wasn't allowed. They knew that every time they smoked or drank they were lying to me, basically saying, "up yours." I admit it. I just sort of believed that I had built relationships with my players—on and off the field; relationships grounded in respect, honesty, and trust. This didn't just anger me, it hurt—and it hurt bad.*

Coach did give Adam some credit. He was the first to come clean and admit that he had been one of those smoking—regularly, and that he had hosted the party where things had gotten out of hand.

> *I did respect the fact that Adam owned up to his part, but I'm not sure anything much changed. In the end there wasn't a lot we could do. Obviously, since it never happened around us we couldn't "prove" anything. And as much as this bugs me, I'm not sure we'd have had the guts to do a lot anyway. It's pretty darn hard to get kids you care about in trouble. Part of me wishes the police had shown up that night and hauled Adam and the whole bunch off to the station. Maybe that would have scared them more—maybe he'd still be alive.*

Book Four

Mr. Mac and Adam

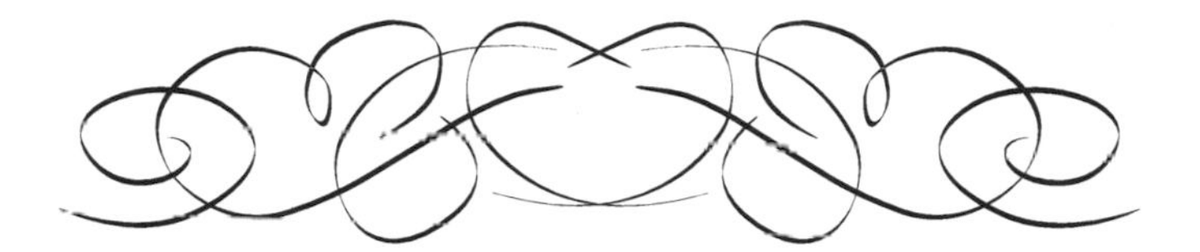

Chapter 1: Mr. Mac and Adam the Son

With Jenny's help I recently discovered two letters that Adam wrote to his father during his sophomore year in high school. His father was a topic that had never come up in our conversations so I learned a lot as I read those letters, and I wondered a great deal about the man who had fathered him. How do you walk away from a child you helped create? How do you not be involved in any way in that child's life, help potty train him, take him to see the Red Sox, go to his football games, teach him to fish, show him how to shave, help him get ready for prom? How do you make the conscious decision to *walk away*, to not do *any* of those things with your own son?

Dear Joe,

Hello, this is your son Adam Routhier. I know this may seem odd, but I looked up some information over the Internet about you and found an address and other stuff. So I decided I would write you a letter, and hopefully get a letter back. I am 15 years old right now; I will be turning 16 in July, on the 17th. I am about 5 feet 11 inches, have dark brown hair and brown eyes. I play football for the Somersworth Toppers; I am a tight end on offense and a safety on defense. I also snowboard; I have been doing that for almost three years now. I like playing video games, or watching football on TV. My favorite football team is the San Francisco 49ers, but they just lost in the playoffs to the Packers and that kind of upset me. That's pretty much everything about me that I enjoy doing and what I look like. I know this must be weird, and maybe you don't want to hear from me, but I have spent my entire life wondering about you, and what you were like, and when my sister found this information for me I decided that I had to at least write you a letter to see if I could find out a little about you. I know that we don't really know each other, but if you could just write a letter back telling me a little about you that would be really great. Thank you.

Sincerely,
Your Son, Adam

* * *

Dear dad,

I am very sorry for the delay in the writing of this letter, it is just that I have been swamped with homework and projects lately, and this is the first real time I have not been doing work. School is kind of a bore sometimes and it can get very annoying when I get this much work, but it's not that bad I guess. There is so much I want to ask you, umm, what do you do for work? Are you married? How old are you? There is just so much on my mind. I was going through some letters and stuff that you sent back when the whole court thing was going on and just got to thinking about many things. I hope you don't mind me typing, it's just that I have very poor hand writing and didn't want to have to worry about you not being able to understand what I am writing. I am going to be turning 16 this July I am so excited. I know it's far away but it is on the top of my thoughts at this moment. I want a car so bad, but I will most likely have to wait for a little bit because I am not able to get any jobs because no one around here wants to hire a 15 and a half year old, it's all 16 year olds. When I turn 16 this summer I am planning to get a job at Walmart because one of the teachers at my school is a manager there and said he would give me a job once I am old enough, but I am not sure how that will work out, because we have a new football coach this year, and he will most likely have double session practices. That will suck, but I think it will be for the better. Maybe you could make it to a couple of games this year if you are not doing anything. I would like to get to start seeing you soon. Maybe if we talk a little bit more and get to know more we could arrange some kind of meeting. I wouldn't want it to be through a court, though, because that would be too much trouble. My mom gets kind of worried sometimes when I tell her I receive letters from you, because she thinks I am going to leave her for you, but I tell her not to worry. Sometimes I get kind of worried about her because she is always so depressed. Do you have any other children, and if so how old are they? Sometimes I get so depressed when I think about not growing up with a father. I mean at least now I can talk to you and hopefully start to see you. It's not like you are dead or anything, but it just kind of sucks. Did you play any sports when you were in high school, and if so what sports? My mom got her job back at the Navy Yard. She applied for a re-instatement or some junk like that and they hired her back, so that's kind of cool. If you have a computer or something, and a way to access the Internet my e-mail address is Bomb266416@aol.com. You are probably wondering why the weird name, but my friends used to call me AdamBomb, so I decided to make that my screen name. I have been typing so much, but I can't seem to stop, there is just so much I want to talk about. I have one of those Playstation 2 things, and it is so incredible. I mean the things they can do with electronics now a days is incredible. I mean the videos in the game look like real people; it's just an amazing thing. I have an obsession with buying movies. I think I have like 60 right now. Movies and video games are pretty much my life right now. I had a girl friend for almost a year but lately things haven't been working out with us so I broke up with her. That was kind of rough, but it was for the best. The other day we had career day at the high school and I talked to this guy from the Army's Airborne division and some of the things he was telling us were incredible. That greatly improved my odds of joining the military. I mean you can make great money and you get to blow stuff up. I don't think it gets any better than that. I try not to think about my future sometimes though because then I get to thinking about all this stuff I want to happen that is going to be incredibly hard to do. I am a very big dreamer, and it can be fun at times but other times it sucks, because stuff like that hardly ever comes true for people. I am pretty excited because football season starts in about 5 months. I have been working out a lot. I am about 5'11 right now but hope to be 6'1 by next year. If I could grow a little bit more before the season I would definitely have the starting tight end spot. I mean right now I am trying to picture what you look like. I mean, how tall are you and stuff? Man I have been typing now for almost 20 minutes and can't seem to stop, but I must because I am about to eat and then go and drop off this letter at the post office, so I can't wait to hear from you again.

Your Son,
Adam

Chapter 2: Mr. Mac and Adam the Student

Along with those letters, I also discovered a draft of Adam's first paper for my philosophy course. It was on Metaphysics—a unit of the course where we study and discuss the nature of reality: what is real and how we make that determination. For example, one of the in-class writing assignments asks students to look at a rock (something theoretically thousands of years old), a skeleton (used to represent the human body), a heart shape (to represent love), and a plant (to represent something living) and write a one-page response about the one they think is the most *real*. We also talk about the dichotomy of the human condition, or more precisely whether or not such a duality—body and soul—even exists, and how or if God factors into this condition.

The longer paper for the unit, two to four pages, asked students to reflect on the philosophers we looked at, our class discussions, readings and videos, and then explore their own personal beliefs about the nature of reality. Even though I am an English teacher, I couldn't read Adam's paper for grammar or proper syntax. I couldn't really read it for continuity or flow or correct punctuation and capitalization either. In all honesty the construction was pretty bad . . . but the content was terrific. So I read it for the content. I read it for the thoughts and ideas it presented, the questions it posed, the possibilities it explored, the emotions it revealed, and the pain it didn't quite conceal.

Routhier 1

Adam Routhier

Intro. To Philosophy

Mr. Mackenzie

Metaphysics Paper

What Is The Matrix?

What is real? Wow what a concept, I mean how is anyone to know whether what we live and experience is reality or just a dream world created by machines. The matrix is one of my favorite movies ever and I have always wondered if that could possibly be true. I honestly feel that we do not live in a false world, but I am not saying it is completely impossible to be true.

I hate the concept that this is all there really is, I mean I truly wish the matrix would be true, I need that kind of excitement in my life. I can't just go through day by day knowing that in about 70 or 80 years I will just be dead, I want to know that my life had some kind of meaning. If it could be possible that I am sitting in a tank where my actual self is connected to the matrix and I am just a figment of some computer then I would like to get out of here as

Routhier 2

soon as possible. I mean right now, as I sit here typing I am chewing some munch 'ems, and if these are just objects that the matrix is telling me are incredibly good then I would like to know that right this instant.

When I first joined this class I must admit that I was not really a very open person, I was strong with my beliefs, but being in this class hearing what everyone has to say has really made me turn into more of an open-minded person. I would have never thought twice that more then just humans and animals could inhabit this world, but now, I am beginning to believe that maybe there may be some intelligent life forms other then us. I also never would have questioned the whole united states landing on the moon, but after hearing it in this class I am not so sure anymore about that either. This class has, I think, changed me for the better.

Anyways though, back to the supporting of the Matrix, look at some of the facts in the Matrix that support the fact we could befake, I mean obviously, somewhere there is someone who is running the show, whether its god, or an agent, or some machine there has to

Routhier 3

be something running the show somewhere. My heritage would have me believe god is the one pulling the strings, but as I grow older and become more of a realist I am starting to wonder if there even can be a god. I mean, is it possible for a single being to have just created the world in seven days, if you ask me I say that is completely ludicrous, but then again, we have no better ideas. If there is such a thing as god, I really hope I get to meet the man some day.

The matrix is a movie that not only entertains the mind, but also kind of challenges it in the same aspect. When I first saw the matrix I just saw it as an awesome action movie with incredible special effects, but in getting older and wiser I now view that movie as an entirely new idea. It really starts you in thinking if our mind and body can be two different things. Getting more into the idea of force and matter of yourself, I think it is such a hard comparison that I really can't judge it. To believe that a movie, of all things can be true is crazy in an aspect, but in another aspect it is completely sane. Which life is real, the life we live, or the life our body lives? I

Routhier 4

often find myself scared of some of the questions we are asked, because if they can be true then I would be astounded. I am open-minded, but I am also concrete, I like things to be described and presented to me if I am going to believe in them. I know living like that is not the best way to live, but it is just so hard to believe it. If I had to find out that my family, and my friends, and my girlfriend were all just images that are presented to me by a machine, then I would not be able to live with myself. It is such a scary thought to think about. I mean and if there is someone creating us all, is it the absolute being who created the earth?

Absolute beings are also quite out there in my aspects. From my catholic heritage, god is the creator of all; he is what's out there for us. But in my logical standpoint, what is god; god is merely just an idea that was created to give people hope. Mainly the reason why I am such a diluted believer in god is the fact that many nights I have prayed for things to get better, and see no results. If there really were a god who really was the ultimate being, he would have answered my prayers in my time of need. You see, that's why you

Routhier 5

can't believe in something there is no proof of. It makes no sense to believe in a person that for all we know could be a tree. On a scientific standpoint I will believe in god, and heaven and hell when there is actual proof of it. I know what I am saying goes completely against my religion, but I have nothing left. Religion has left me just as sad as relationships, and tragedies. For a long part of my life, I tried to recline on religion to sooth my pain, and it did absolutely nothing for me. Religion, the absolute being, and two different worlds, some may think they are completely different, but I say they have just as much in common as shoes and socks. If there are two different worlds then that would be devastating to the religious community, that would mean that any and all religious thoughts are false. And if there are two different worlds then how could there possibly be an absolute being? It is questions like this that probe my mind and find me in search of answers that I know I will most likely never find.

* * *

You have just read Adam's own unrevised and unedited composition. I hope you read it the same way I did, for the emotion clearly poured into it and the humanity it so poignantly displayed. Otherwise you'll have missed everything in it that's important.

Book Five

Mr. Mac and . . .

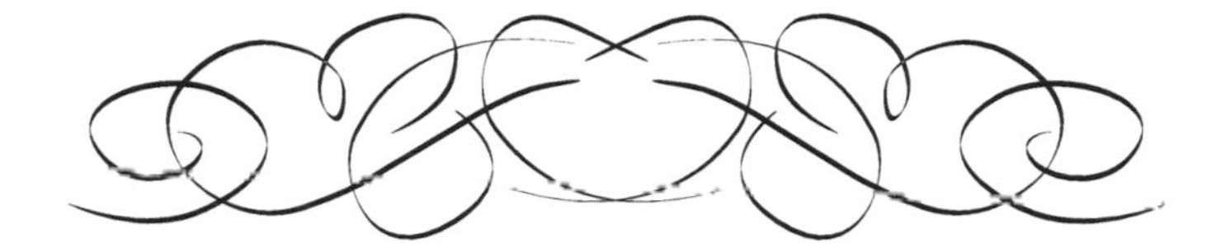

Chapter 1: Mr. Mac

It's still so vivid, like the memory of my first grade teacher telling us that President Kennedy had been shot and we were being dismissed from school. Or like how I can still see myself in my Oldsmobile Cutlass Supreme making the turn on the entrance ramp to Rt. 128 from the Liberty Tree Mall in Danvers, MA. The radio was on and I heard, "We have a major malfunction" with the Challenger. On the driveway right behind my Toyota pick-up lay the daily *Foster's.* I can still see that headline "Man Killed In Crash" and feel my body go kind of numb as I read.

See, I'm a guy who likes to fix things for my students, who is most comfortable making things better or at least easier to bear: buy a bus ticket for Justine, who had no money to go visit her father at Christmas; extend a paper deadline for Rachel who was dealing with leukemia treatments; go to the funeral home when Josh and Garry's brother-in-law died. There was no way to "fix" this. Nothing I could buy or extend or visit. And what made it even worse was that I had to put down the newspaper, pull myself together enough to call Charlene, and then go direct the choir which was singing in a city-wide 9/11 memorial service that morning at Henry Law Park in Dover.

Charlene was barely functional but she did come to the phone and we were both crying as we tried to talk. She said she was glad I had called because she'd been having trouble finding my number and she wanted to talk with me. She said she and her family would really like it if I would give the eulogy at Adam's memorial service. She said they had all loved my speech at graduation in June and one of the first things they had decided was to ask me to do this. My mind was swirling with *I can't possibly manage that,* as my mouth said, "Charlene, I will do absolutely anything you want me to." She thanked me and I said I'd be over as soon as I got home from Dover. Then we hung up. My wife and I headed to Dover. *I can't believe I have to go sit through a church service in this condition.*

All around me speakers are remembering the victims of the attack on the World Trade Center: the workers, firefighters, police, emergency responders, all of their families. I'm thinking about Charlene and Jenny and all of Adam's friends—people who I know are in an even more immediate agony.

> "Today we are gathered to pay tribute . . .
>
> *How can Charlene possibly be coping . . . Oh my God, Meme . . .*
>
> ". . . we pray for all the people whose lives were devastated . . .
>
> *How will Steven ever survive this, and Austin and DJ and . . .*
>
> ". . . we even pray for those who perpetrated this devastating attack . . .
>
> *This can't possibly be happening . . . his whole life was in front of him. . . dear God, how can I bear this . . .*
>
> ". . . O gracious God, for all these people we pray. Amen."
>
> *My kids, oh my God, my kids . . .*

I got to Adam's house around noon and sat and cried and hugged family members for more than an hour. I heard them say nice things to me that I didn't really deserve. Meme said, "You were always there for him and he knew it." And Faye remarked, "You are the only man I ever saw Adam hug except for my father." And somewhere in there Charlene said, "I hope it's okay that we listed you as a survivor in the obituary." And all the while my tears barely even slowed down.

I combed through dozens of pictures that had been assembled on the kitchen table—many of which had been taken just a scant three months before at graduation. There was my Adam, in one picture after another, happy, handsome, and as full of life as ever: smiling and standing tall between Charlene and Jenny; the Adam grin with Austin; looking oh so studly with Meme in his cap and gown, unzipped and showing his white wife-beater; wrapping me up in a huge bear hug on the football field following graduation.

Charlene mentioned that a bunch of the kids had been by and she thought they had gone over to Joey's house, so that's where I headed next. I parked up on the street and began walking down a long curved driveway. Almost as soon as I started walking, I heard someone say, "Hey, I think that's Mr. Mac," and I saw Joey start moving towards me.

Maybe thirty feet from me, as we both kept walking, he said "I knew you'd come, I knew it." By fifteen feet, we could see each other's tears running—hard tears. At two feet, our arms went out and we pulled each other through the last inches into a tight embrace. We stood there, our chests heaving, our hearts breaking, convulsing with each sob.

Chapter 2: Mrs. Drew

That summer Mrs. Drew's mother had been sick and she was trying to keep up with her garden. Since they couldn't possibly eat everything she grew, she brought vegetables over to the Routhiers' quite a lot. She would frequently see Adam when she stopped in and he would always chat for a few minutes. She commented to herself on several occasions that he had turned out to be a pretty good kid.

The night of the accident she came home from work via Main Street from Rollinsford rather than across Green Street and down Indigo Hill Road, so she didn't see any lights or police cars or emergency vehicles. Maybe around 6pm a neighbor called to tell her that Adam had been in a car accident and had died at the scene. The shock and sadness she felt was overwhelming. Tears—immediately. The neighbor gave her as much information as she knew but none of it felt real. It just didn't seem possible. Then she thought of her son Josh and that she was going to have to call and tell him. He was up at Plymouth State College just beginning his first semester. He'd been home the weekend before and had spent a lot of time at Adam's. She called his cell but could immediately tell from his voice that he already knew. Everyone up there had heard. Selfishly, she was relieved she didn't have to be the one to tell him. He told her he'd be home the next morning. She emailed Chris, who by then was in the Navy and out to sea. She also called her mother and her ex-husband to let them know as well.

Finally, with nothing left to do, she walked over to the Routhiers'. A crowd of Adam's friends were hanging out on the front lawn. She went inside and talked with Charlene and Meme for about a half hour or so. They were all still in shock and disbelief. They talked about all the family coming in. Mrs. Drew offered to lend them a blow up mattress for the next week or so.

> *The next morning I thought I was having a heart attack. I had chest pains that just would not go away. I finally went to the hospital and was admitted for several*

hours. They gave me all the appropriate heart tests but ultimately the doctors diagnosed it as severe anxiety. The combination of all the stress with my mother's illness, Adam's accident, worrying about Josh and his reaction, and feeling so bad for Charlene, was more than my mind and body could handle. I kept seeing the dents in my door, the mini fire out back, "Ultimate Adam" splashing around in my swimming pool. I kept seeing Charlene and feeling the grief and pain that only a mother can truly know.

Josh was one of the pall bearers and one of the group that got a tattoo of Adam's initials on his shoulder. Austin, who worked for Somersworth Hot 'N Fast, arrived at the Drew house one evening shortly after the accident to deliver a pizza. It was a really cold day but he stood there on the front steps and took off his tee shirt to show Mrs. Drew the tattoo. For several years after that, any time he delivered pizza to her house, they talked about Charlene and how she was doing.

Sometime after the accident she and Josh went through a bunch of old albums and made copies of some of their favorite photos of Josh and Adam. Josh brought some of them over to Adam's room. His mom still takes hers out every so often and smiles at that mischievous grin and feels so sad.

Nearly ten years later I still avoid driving down Indigo Hill whenever possible, almost always opting to go in and out of Somersworth by way of Green Street or Main Street. Very rarely do I forget and go by the accident site but I think of Adam every single time I turn in my street and go by his house. Someone else lives there now, but that hasn't stopped me from thinking of him running around my house, climbing on the furniture, breaking things, building forts, firing off rockets, and answering for it all with one of his Adam smiles.

Chapter 3: DJ

Then came the night that changed all of our lives. The biggest reason I am who I am. The reason I'm looking back on football games and practices, the Tire-Tanic, bike rides, and sleep overs, and Madden, and so much of my life, and still feeling sad. The reason I know that when I think about these things I'll always be sad, even if I live to be a hundred.

I was attending my first actual party at UNH. The place was known on campus as "the greens" and it was a place where every person on campus was welcome. I remember going there with a couple of new friends and bumped into an old friend, Kelsey. She lived in Somersworth but went to a different high school than the rest of our group. Still, she was always one of us and I was pretty close with her, especially because of her connection with Ruth. As the night went on we were drinking and partying, having a grand ole time. It was a Friday night and I had plenty of drinks to be sure I made friends with everyone there.

There I was, in a sea of underage drinkers, when all of a sudden I heard hysterical crying and someone came up and hugged me. Trying to keep my balance and not slop my drink, I realized it was Kelsey. She only had enough strength to say three words, "DJ, it's Adam." I held her close and could tell by her tears that something horrible had happened. I grabbed her hand and walked her outside. She kind of mumbled under her breath, "Adam is dead. He was in a car crash."

My first thoughts were, "What the hell is she talking about? When she says Adam does she mean Ruth? I just saw Ruth earlier this week. Holy shit, I need to call

Austin." I asked her, "Are you sure? Where did you hear this? Oh my God, let's get the fuck out of here."

Kelsey could barely walk she was so upset. I don't even remember where we went but I remember walking with her to a small grassy hill just outside of the party zone. We sat there crying for ten or fifteen minutes before some of Kelsey's friends showed up. They took Kelsey back to her dorm and I just started walking.

While I walked to nowhere I called everyone I could think of. The first one was Austin, who was still at the scene of the accident with Steven. He confirmed what Kelsey had told me, and that was when it became real life. I called Joey, Evan and Tim, who were all at Plymouth State, and they confirmed it as well. It all seemed fake. I kept wondering how, why, when and if I was the last person on earth to find out.

In reality I found out only minutes after it happened but I felt like I had been left out of life-changing news and was playing catch up to everyone else. I walked around campus talking on the phone with anyone who would pick up. I went through the phone book in the middle of the night and tried to get a hold of all my closest friends. As much as I wanted to, I remember not calling my parents—because I didn't want them to know I'd been drinking.

After what seemed like hours walking around and periodically sitting by myself and crying at various spots around campus, I made it back to my room. My roommate Jed was awake playing guitar. When he asked what was the matter, I told him the news and he was shocked. We were still practically strangers but I could tell by the look on his face how sorry he was. I climbed up into bed and cried myself to sleep that night. The next morning I remember getting a ride to Joey's house and seeing everyone who could be there. Friends who I had just said goodbye to and didn't think I would be seeing again until Thanksgiving break. It was way too soon to be getting together. I remember Mr. Mac coming over just to be with us, and hug us, and cry with us. It didn't make things okay but it made them better. The next few weeks were the hardest of my life.

Chapter 4: Jenny

I don't have a clue how I survived it. I had graduated from the University of Maine at Farmington in May and worked the 2004 summer on an island in Belgrade. When the season ended I picked up some part-time hours back at UMF in the dining hall. That day I had worked a banquet. I had been there for about ten hours, staying late to help in the dish room. We had the music cranked up really loud and were singing and dancing. I stopped at Dunkin' Donuts for an iced coffee on my way home because it was so freakin' hot. When I got to my apartment, my boyfriend and I plopped down in front of a fan and started watching our favorite show, CSI. Around 10:00 the phone rang, but we didn't answer it. Fifteen minutes later there was a knock at the door.

We were both in our underwear because of the heat and so while Darren answered the door in his boxers, I ran to put some clothes on. Darren came into the bedroom and said that someone from the police department was there and wanted to talk to me. As I was getting dressed I started feeling angry thinking that someone had done something to my car which was parked across the street. They told me that my brother had been involved in an accident and didn't make it. I asked what happened and they said he was on a motorcycle. My brain couldn't comprehend that. My brother didn't drive a motorcycle. They called the Somersworth Police Department to clarify that it had been a motor vehicle accident. I remember thinking that since they were wrong about the motorcycle, they must be wrong about this too. It was someone else. A mix-up.

I remember words coming out of my mouth as I talked to the officers but I have no recollection of what I said. It was like my body had detached from any motor skills. I picked up my cell phone to call my family and couldn't remember any numbers. I couldn't get the phone to dial. I tried three or four times, needing to talk to someone. I finally got my Tante Faye on the phone and she told me there had been an accident. I was 130 miles away from my family. Two friends from college came over while I was sitting paralyzed in front of my computer. Adam had an "away message" up on AIM that said he was at the mall. I remember saying that out loud. "My brother is at the mall." I remember the look my friends gave me, powerless, helpless, relief that it wasn't their brother.

My friends drove my boyfriend and me to his parents' house, which was an hour away, and then they drove us to New Hampshire. I sat sunken into the bucket seat of the van going back and forth. Is this real? The energy around me was weird. I tried to process the idea that my brother had died. Tried to imagine existing on this earth without him. My brain was trying to tell me that I was in a dream—a nightmare—but my body told me otherwise.

When we got to my house in Somersworth, I don't remember getting from the van to the front door but I remember freezing just before the entry way. I started to cry out and my body wouldn't move any further. The house no longer felt safe to me. I couldn't go in. I just stood there as people told me it was going to be okay and forced me through the doorway and into the kitchen. I can't even tell you who was there besides my mom, Meme, and Tante Faye. I didn't want anyone around me. I just wanted to be left alone. It was really late and people eventually went off to bed. I stayed on the couch bundled up in a blanket trying to watch TV. I couldn't. My aunt came out to talk to me and somehow we ended up at the site of the accident. There were candles, and trinkets, and I saw some notes. I cried, asked a lot of questions, and cried some more. As we stood there a police officer drove by and questioned us. He didn't want us to stay long because it was dark out and dangerous. No kidding.

Chapter 5: Tim

Without a doubt the worst night of my life. It was freshmen year of college and Evan, Joey, and I had all made the trek to Plymouth State University in Plymouth, New Hampshire. Josh had decided late to go as well. It was a Friday night and classes had just started two weeks prior, so everyone was still in that getting-to-know-people mode. Josh, Joey, and I all went over to our friend Chad's room to have a few pre-game beers before we went out that night. We were going across campus to a high lighter party. You're supposed to wear a white t-shirt and everyone then writes on you in highlighter. We'd been told it's a lot of fun and pretty crazy when there are only black lights on.

We pounded down what we had left of the beer and started our walk across campus. It was only about a ten-minute walk, straight through the center of campus to the other side. We couldn't have been walking more than about five minutes, maybe halfway there, maybe a little less. We were all pretty buzzed. Anyway I remember being out front of the HUB, our recreation building, when Joey's phone rang. I didn't think anything of it and just kept walking with everyone else. Then I heard Joey talking into the phone in this weird, serious voice I barely recognized. "NO, you're kidding me? Tell me you're kidding with me. Don't mess around with me like this." We all stopped as we heard him talking and knew it had to be important judging by his look and audible reactions. He then looked up at me and Evan and said two words that froze us stiff, two words that will never make sense to me. "Ruth's dead."

We had already stopped walking and we just sat down on the grass, I guess to talk, except no one was actually talking. "This isn't real," I thought to myself. "Someone's fucking with us. Ruth's fucking with us." I remember thinking that in my head. But as Joey got off the phone, he started talking to us about how that was Austin. He said he was at the scene and could hardly understand him 'cause he was bawling his eyes out while he'd been talking. He said that they'd already pronounced him dead. By the time he got off the phone we knew there was no denying it. One of our best friends was dead. The three of us just sat there staring at each other in utter disbelief, three bodies sitting on the ground trying to figure out what the fuck to do next. I mean what do you do when your life has just been shattered? What do you do? What do you say? Who do you say it to? Moms? Dads? God? What the fuck? How did this happen? What are we supposed to fucking do?

For maybe a half hour, but it could have been more, we just sat there crying, picking grass, shredding it, picking more. Eventually we moved to a bench on Alumni Green so we could be more by ourselves and cried. We tried to talk. We tried to stop crying. We tried to do the impossible, make sense out of something that was totally senseless. So we sat, mostly in silence, mentally replaying the one-sided phone call that had just destroyed our world. And cried.

Chapter 6: Andy

I was just going over to my friend Micha's house to hang out. We had barely walked in the door when Micha got a call and told me Adam had been in a really bad accident on Indigo Hill Road. I remember thinking, no way, I was just on Indigo Hill. But I realized I had turned in the opposite direction of the accident. I jumped back into my car to go see what had happened. On the way my mind started swirling . . .

My senior year had been pretty awkward. I didn't spend any time at all with those guys—Steven, DJ, Austin, Ruth. Not once. We didn't have football anymore and they had never called me to hang out. I had even tried my hardest to pick classes they weren't in so it didn't feel so weird. It was like we'd never been friends at all. Right through graduation. They hadn't been mean to me exactly, more like I just didn't exist anymore.

Then, about two weeks before I was headed off to college, Ruth had called and asked me if I wanted to hang out. It's not that we did anything too fantastic but it was the first time in like two years that he had called. We went over to Hilltop Fun Center and played a few games in the arcade and then hit a few balls in the batting cages. Then we just drove around for a while.

The thing is, I couldn't have cared less what we did. We could have done nothing. Just his phone call had validated me. Asking me if I wanted to hang out, it was like he had told me that our old friendship still mattered. That I still mattered.

I hardly remember arriving at the accident scene, but right away my worst fears confirmed. I looked for Steven but didn't see him. I walked around crying and hugging friends. I moved between worrying about Steven and feeling sorry for myself. God, this can't be happening! I never told Ruth how much that call and that afternoon meant to me. I just never thought to tell him. And now I can't.

Chapter 7: Joey

We used to live like we were invincible. We never thought about anything bad happening to us. We never feared, never even thought of consequences. It was an ignorant way to live. I was on my way to a party in Plymouth with Tim, Evan, Josh, and a few other friends when I got the call that changed my life. It was Steven letting me know that there had been an accident and that Ruth was gone. I just remember kind of collapsing when I realized the seriousness of his voice, knowing he wasn't just screwing with me. I was crying before I hit the ground, and I remember having a hard time breathing and people trying to help me. I just refused to believe he was gone. I had just talked with him about coming up to visit and about how much fun we would have. I felt like my life was like his. Over.

The first call I made was to my mother who was on a trip visiting family in Pennsylvania. I could barely speak. When I finally got it out that Adam had been in a car crash and was dead, her breakdown only contributed to my hysteria. So much of my education, my athletics, my friendships—Christ, my life—was wrapped up in him. How the Hell was I supposed to go on living with him gone? It was all so damned unfair. I mean, maybe in some way we deserved a huge wake-up call to the way we were living our lives, but no one deserves to die. Especially not Ruth. I mean, I think we all knew that he was the one everybody loved the most. I guess it was because of how vulnerable he was beneath all of that laughter and bravado. Those of us who really knew him knew what he'd been through. Growing up without a dad and his mom having to deal with her own demons. If you hung out at Ruth's house you knew what he was all about. Good times and true enjoyment of the moment. And how he was with his mom and sister. Very protective.

With those feelings of loss, anger, sadness, fear, I had to face the days after, including the funeral. I remember having pretty much everyone from our crowd over at my house the day following the accident. There were so many people there, just like there had been on lots of occasions. But the life of the party wasn't among them. The center of attention who always made everybody laugh wasn't there . . . and no one was laughing. I remember seeing Mr. Mac walking down my driveway and I went to meet him. I knew how much he cared about Ruth, and seeing that on his face was so painful. I don't know how long we stood there hugging each other. There was one kind of odd thing I remember feeling. Seeing how many people cared about Ruth and were now mourning him was heart-breaking, but it was kind of moving, too. I felt a sense of pride to have been best friends with someone who so many people loved.

I remember very little about the funeral. Just having to carry the casket down the aisle of the church was so hard. Most of the service and the burial I couldn't tell you much about, really. The whole day was kind of a blur. I do remember looking at his family and seeing how distraught his mom and Meme were. One thing that kept me going was telling myself that I needed to be there for them going forward. That day wasn't about me and my pain. It wasn't even about Ruth. He would have wanted me there all right, but not for him. For his family.

Chapter 8: Steven

I don't even know where to begin about that day. He called me on my cell, Ruth I mean. We made plans to meet up when he got back from the mall, only. . . yeah. I think it was about 8:00 when Austin called me. I was at the football game, or maybe I hadn't gotten there yet. I think we were all supposed to meet up at the high school to see the game. Maybe. I can't quite remember.

But I do remember that Austin called and said there'd been an accident. He seemed pretty worked up, said something like that he thought it might be Ruth. I guess Nicole had called him and said her uncle had been listening to a police scanner when this thing about an accident over on Indigo Hill came over it and the description of the car sounded kind of like Ruth's, or something like that. He sounded pretty upset and he wasn't making a lot of sense but he told me he'd meet me at the high school and we'd drive over together. I remember feeling weird, like scared weird.

It's funny, I can hardly remember the ride over there. We went in Austin's car. I remember seeing flashing lights in the distance from fire trucks and police cars and we could hear scratchy broken voices talking over intercoms or scanners or something. We got out of the car and started to walk towards the lights and I remember they got brighter. Like they were everywhere, flashing lights on all the emergency vehicles and flares on both sides of the accident and flood lights in the woods. Christ, the place was lit up like, like a night game at Fenway Park or my living room on Christmas Eve. Like you could hardly tell it was night out. And then I saw something that really scared me.

"Dude, I think that's Charlene over there. It is her." And we worked our way towards where she was standing. And then I noticed our priest standing with them. But then I thought I overheard somebody say something about broken legs, so I'm like okay, well, that's not so bad. But that thought was immediately replaced with what felt like a gunshot or a knife to my gut. I almost fell down as I heard a policeman say to Charlene, "I'm sorry for your loss . . ." What loss? This can't be happening! He told me he was going to the mall and we'd meet up afterward. We're supposed to go to the football game. What the fuck is happening? He was just going to the fucking mall. Don't do this to us. Don't you fucking do this, you motherfucker.

Sometimes, looking back I wonder who I was talking to. Ruth? God? The Devil? I wanted to puke. I wanted to be with him. Some days . . . part of me still does.

Chapter 9: Charlene

The last thing I heard Adam say as he was heading out the door was, "I'm going to the Mall." A couple hours later I received a phone call from my mother. She was visiting with my cousin Danny who lived right in Somersworth and had a police scanner. My mother first asked me what Adam's license plate number was, but I didn't know. She told me that they heard of an accident on Indigo Hill Road and she wasn't sure if it was Adam. After I hung up the phone, something told me to get in the car and drive down the road. I had to make sure it wasn't Adam. I jumped in the car. I think I was barefoot. I drove down Indigo Hill. I saw a lot of commotion on the left side of the road and pulled over and parked. I couldn't quite believe what I saw. Adam's car by a tree in the woods. I also saw Adam sitting in the driver seat. I only saw him from behind. He was just sitting there.

It's hard to explain what I felt, because I can't be sure I was feeling. One second I didn't believe it was Adam, and the next second I knew it was. He was just going to the mall. People don't die going to the mall. I started walking up the road so I could ask someone if they knew what happened. I remember one woman said a man in a truck was racing and his truck went off the road. I felt a sigh of relief thinking it couldn't be Adam, it was a man in a truck. The relief only lasted a few seconds, though, because in my mind I kept seeing Adam sitting in his car by the tree. At first it was real, and then it wasn't real. He was only going to the mall. I didn't know what was happening.

The road started to get full of people. I vaguely remember saying to some woman standing there, "I think that's my son, I think that's my son." I think she held my hand. There was a police officer standing a few feet away and I said the same thing to him. "I think that's my son." He asked me why I thought that and what my son's name was. I told him I saw a car that looked just like his. He asked me what kind of car it was and whose name it was in. I told him it was a Chevy Cavalier and it was in my name, and my son is Adam Routhier. I'll never forget those words from the police officer. He said, "Ma'am, it is your son and he is deceased."

I don't know what happened to me after I heard those words. I think my whole body went into some kind of shock. I kept thinking, "This is not real, but it is real. This is not happening, but it is happening." The only way I can explain how I felt is that I was in the Twilight Zone, but I can't explain that either. I just wanted to grab the officer's gun and shoot myself.

Finally the officer took me to his car and asked if there was someone he could call for me. I wanted my mother to be there, but I didn't want her to find out that it was Adam who was in the accident. The officer also asked me if I wanted a priest or anything. I thought about Father Aaron at St. Martin's Church. They called him and he came right down. A group of us held hands and prayed. I saw my mother arrive. She had her hand over her mouth and was crying.

Jenny was living in Farmington, Maine, at the time. The Somersworth police gave a message to the Farmington Police to tell Jenny about her brother. When she finally made it home, she was crying hysterically. I think she was afraid to come into the house at first. It was just an awful night. The police called Victims, Inc. and they came over to be with us. They're an organization that helps families when someone passes away. I remember sitting at the kitchen table and all these kids starting coming in and giving me hugs. They were friends of Adam's. It really did help me to have them there . . . but it wasn't the same. That night I slept with Meme and Jenny in Meme's room. At least I think I did.

Nothing's ever been the same since that night.

Adam and I had the same sense of humor. We sometimes watched Seinfeld and Saturday Night Live together and would just laugh.

Sometimes I wonder if I should have been stricter with him—would he . . .

What if I hadn't let Joe drive me to drink—literally. Would I have been a stronger person? A better mother?

Even that's not really fair, blaming my problems on Joe. I just can't help but wonder . . .

Adam really didn't talk to me about Joe. He and Jenny got together on that. I did see the picture that Joe sent him. I think Adam kept it in his wallet.

One day when some of the guys came over—I think it was Austin and Steven, maybe Jake too, not sure, I told them they could have anything of Adam's as a keepsake. Except the TV. I think one of the guys took Adam's wallet as a memento. I forgot to tell them TV and wallet. I didn't notice it was gone until a day or two later. I wanted to keep his wallet. I'm not upset with anyone or anything. It's just that I wanted to keep it. Oh, well, that's okay.

Even now, sometimes I still think, "He was just going to the mall."

Nothing has ever been the same.

Chapter 10: Mr. Mac

St. Martin's Church, September 15, 2004

Eulogy for
Adam Routhier

Forever Grateful

The last time I stood before most of you to speak was this past June at the class of 2004's graduation from Somersworth High School. It was a joyous occasion with a message of hope and encouragement.

The last time I spoke in this sanctuary I was speaking in support of Pete Houde at his Eagle Scout Court of Honor.

The first time I spoke in this sanctuary was in support of Adam Pope at *his* Eagle Scout Court of Honor, all with messages of hope and encouragement. They were easier messages to deliver. Yet, Lord knows, today we are in pretty serious need of hope and encouragement.

Those of you who know me best know I don't run a very conventional classroom. In my role as a church musician I've never given a very conventional concert. I've been told I don't deliver a very conventional commencement address, and you may not find this to be a very conventional eulogy, although going back to the word's Latin root *eulogium*, meaning "praise," I actually intend this to be a textbook example of a eulogy.

I brought a few things with me today—I hope you don't mind. Think of them as pieces of my security blanket: My 2004 yearbook with Adam's picture in it, the miracle jar from my desk, and the sign I silently read—rather than yell—on those rare occasions when I get particularly frustrated.

Since you can't hear my mind, today I'll read it aloud:

ON TEACHING

I've come to a frightening conclusion that I am the
decisive element in the classroom.
It's my personal approach that creates the climate.
It's my daily mood that makes the weather.

As a teacher, I possess a tremendous power to make a
child's life miserable or joyous. I can be a tool of
torture or an instrument of inspiration.
I can humiliate or humor, hurt or heal.
In all situations, it is my response that decides
whether a crisis will be escalated or de-escalated,
and a child humanized or de-humanized.

--Haim Ginott

Adam Routhier was my student. He put up with me for ninety minutes a day for an entire year's worth of his high school career in both Intro to Philosophy and Honors English IV. Much more importantly, Adam Routhier was my friend. I loved him and he loved me. It's too bad in a way that Adam isn't in one of my classes this year because I've started a new tradition he would like—one I stole from a Baltimore High School football coach. Sometime during most of my class sessions I will ask, "What is my job?" to which my students respond, "To love us!" And I will then query, "And what is your job?" to which they reply, "To love each other!" Adam would like that—I know he would because I remember the last words we spoke to each other, a final verbal exchange for which I will be forever grateful. The photo I'm holding is of Adam and me locked in a tight embrace just following graduation. What you can't hear are the words we spoke: "I love you, Adam Routhier." To which he responded, "I love you too, Mr. Mac."

Make no mistake—Adam was not a teacher's dream scholar. He was highly unmotivated when it came to work, particularly homework. He was a terrible procrastinator. And one of the few days he wasn't chatting too much with Tim or DJ was the day he was keeping score on the number of times I had to say, "Please be quiet," during his block one class. I think the count was something like thirty-six times. So no, Adam was not a teacher's dream scholar, but he was a teacher's dream student. This I know because he was one of my dream students. Adam never, to the best of my recollection, uttered a disrespectful word in my classroom. He was never unkind to anyone in my classroom. He never played the victim, never looked for someone else to blame, and, while he might not always have volunteered the truth, I don't believe he ever told me a lie. He wasn't a perfect kid—just a great one.

Folks, there is nothing I can say, no joke I can tell, no cliché I can retell, not even any original prose I can compose that will take away the pain we are all feeling. I wish there were—I'd tell it or retell it or write it. But maybe together we can explore another dimension or angle of the pain to make it a bit more bearable: friends, the reason it hurts so bad is because we loved him so much—and that is a good thing! I want you to do something. I want you to close your eyes and let some image, some memory of Adam fill your mind—keep 'em closed for just a minute and focus on that image. Now consider this, you would not have that image, that memory, that moment to hold onto for the rest of your life if your life had not been blessed by the presence of Adam. Yes, losing Adam at such a young age is a tragedy, one we will likely never fully understand. But the larger tragedy would be if we had never had him at all.

And, oh, those memories! Steven was talking the other day about the famous Routhier sleep overs: playing video games till four o'clock in the morning, or stumbling downstairs to go home before it was light and trying on shoes out of the pile until they found the ones that fit. Evan was telling me about the long conversations he and Adam used to have—often times about philosophical subjects like the universe, life, death. Evan said, "Ruth always had his own opinion, and since he was smart I usually agreed with him." Then there was Lauren who was telling me about the time she and a bunch of girls ended up in his room together. Adam was the only guy. For some reason the conversation abruptly ended and there was one of those awkward silences. All of a sudden Adam busts out with, "Hey, who wants to make out?" And DJ remembers freshmen year football season when they experienced the "tradition" of getting wacked in the behind with a field hockey stick. Now normally, that was considered pretty embarrassing. Not by Adam, though. See he got wacked by some of the girls on the team and actually came up with a smile on his face saying, "Oh, man! Those girls are so hot." Adam

Routhier was a rich part of our lives, and I would not trade all the agony I feel at this moment for even one single memory of our time together. I don't believe you would either.

I do remember a sadder time, when Adam came to me to ask if we could talk. Life was not going the way he wanted it to and he was beating himself up pretty badly. He sat at my desk and talked and wept. He wasn't happy with the way he was conducting himself, personally or scholastically. He said to me, "Mr. Mac, I feel like such a loser. I have no job, no car, no money. I'm doing terrible at school, I'm in danger of not graduating, and I don't seem to be able to break out of it. I just feel like such a loser." We chatted for a while and I finally asked, "Adam, do you love your mom?" "Definitely." "Do you trust me?" "Mr. Mac, you know I do." "I think it would be helpful, at least to your academics, if the three of us sat down and talked. Clearly, you need some reinforcing and I think we need to enlist your mom's help." He agreed and the three of us had a summit meeting. We didn't solve every problem Adam had, but I will always be grateful that we managed to get him pulled up out of the pits. He got himself together enough to graduate. He got a part-time job and with Mom's help bought a car. Recently he found a full-time job and began making plans to go to college. I believe Adam no longer felt like a loser.

The truth is, in many ways Adam was a winner. Over the last several days I have been privileged to hear a lot of things about him. I've heard Charlene talk about what an incredible son he was. I've seen the photos of Adam and Jenny and listened to her stories about her great brother. Through tears and deep breaths I've heard his grandmother talk about her loving and devoted grandson. I've seen first-hand how much he was loved by his aunts and uncles and cousins. I saw one of his friends pick up the family portrait at the funeral home, the one with a young, blond-streaked Adam standing center and above Mom, Jenny, and Meme, and remark, "this pretty much says it all about Ruth—takin' care of the family."

And oh, the myriad people Adam could count as friends. See, I know they are great friends, because many of them are my friends too. Look around and you'll see who they are—for they are you. You, the people who have provided him a family and a home; the people who have left memorial tokens and flowers and crosses beside the road in remembrance of him; the people who have worked for hours on collages and buttons to memorialize him; the people who have played ball with him, worked with him, taught him, bathed and fed him, laughed and joked with him; the people who played video games and listened to classic rock CDs with him, sat around backyard fires with him, and talked incessantly in class with him; the people who got to school by seven or shortly after most mornings throughout high school just to hang out in the upper hall—*our* hall; the people who have held each other and cried together over the last five days—you are the living legacy of Adam Routhier. Your presence here is beyond overwhelming.

You see, it wasn't just me and Charlene and a few lucky young ladies that Adam embraced. Adam embraced life. As part of their final course assignment I always ask my seniors to write me a short personal letter in which they must, no matter what else they say, comment on how the course impacted them as students. Adam wrote this:

> *Well, I don't know where to begin with you about this course. I started the semester expecting this course to be a life-changing experience and I must say that it really has been. In no way could I have ever expected the level of work to be this hard, and at times I had the biggest urge to just give up and quit. However, on a level aside from school I feel that everything you've helped me through this year has not only helped me for the time being but for the rest of my life. You were there for me through some of the hardest times in my life and for that all I can say is thank you so much and "Love ya, mean it."*
>
> *Sincerely,*
> *Adam Routhier*

There is much for which I will be forever grateful regarding Adam: The image of him sitting on the far side of my classroom, biceps busting out of a polo shirt topped by a white nugget choker; his unique smile—something part smile, part grin, with a dash of smirk; the laughs about how he wrote his S's and 5's from the bottom up. Like this graduation photograph of him and me, I will cherish my memories of

Adam, as I know you will cherish yours. Mostly, at the end, I will be forever grateful for the faith that I can say still, "I love you, Adam Routhier," and know that somewhere he is responding, "I love you too, Mr. Mac."

Love you, Adam.
Mean it.

Epilogue

Somersworth High School Graduation Speech, June 11, 2004

What's It All About?

Will someone please tell me where on Earth the last four years have gone? Do you realize that four years ago you all were eighth graders, worried about freshman initiations, high school algebra, and zits? Close to home, Stroudwater Books was still in business, Walmart had recently taken a cue from McDonald's and super-sized, and gas was about $1.35 a gallon. Here at the high school, Ms. Cardinal had not yet become Mrs. George, Mr. Watson was still trying to teach you how to avoid sexually transmitted diseases, and Garrett was trying to forget about falling into the bio-dome! City Hall was squished into 157 Main Street and the Police department even then was talking about needing a new building—they're still talking about it. Statewide, Governor Shaheen was already looking to become Senator Shaheen, Senator Bob Smith was busy having a national temper tantrum, and the Old Man of the Mountain was still hanging on. Nationally, the Twin Towers were still the nerve center of world trade, Boy Bands were the rage, Beyonce had blossomed through puberty, Jim Jeffords was a Republican, John Kerry's medals were still missing and while Hillary was saying it takes a village, some of us were thinking it takes a mom and a dad. Oh yeah, and Rush Limbaugh was still ranting about Monica, Bill, and that stupid dress.

I am proud to live in the City of Somersworth, proud of Somersworth High School and Regional Vocational Center, and proud to be a member of the faculty here. I am particularly proud of the Class of 2004, and want to thank them for inviting me to be the guest speaker at their graduation. It is truly an honor to be here. Like the others before me, I want to welcome you all and to say a special thank you to all of the parents here today, for not only the opportunity but the privilege of working with your daughters and sons. They have impacted my life in so many ways! I have been awed by some, aghast at others, but have loved them all.

I'm not sure just what it is that connects certain groups of students to certain teachers—or certain teachers to certain groups of students. I do know that the teachers I connected with as a student were not the ones who "taught outside the box," or those who made a "paradigm shift" in pedagogy. They were not the teachers who were "ahead of their time" or those who tried to fill my empty mind with their brilliance. They were the teachers who tried to make me *see* and then *develop* what I already had. Mr. Hudson, my Dover High choral director, who might ask *me* how to play a certain section of the piece we were rehearsing. Third grade's Miss Casey, to whom I will always be grateful for Times Table Bingo. Mrs. Reid who tried desperately to teach a group of incredibly naïve Rollinsford Grade School sixth graders sex education. Mr. Kalishman, who let me bring my 1967 Cadillac on a class field trip to UNH in 1975; of course, only adults could drive! Tamara Niedzolkowski, my UNH English 401 instructor, who was the first teacher I ever heard drop an "F" bomb in class, who cared about what *I* thought, who changed my ideas about teaching and thus my undergraduate major from music to English. It was the teachers who were a little too tall or short, or acted a bit weird, maybe were slightly wacked, not perfectly painted or pressed. It was the teachers who liked their jobs, liked their lives, liked their students.

So what, you might ask, connected me to this group of students? On the first day of class as I began my trip around the room, checking in with each student, I got to this somewhat shy appearing young lady named Stephanie.

"Bragdon," I said. "Are you a Somersworth girl?"

"Yes," she quietly replied, still looking down.

"You got any brothers?

"Two," she responded rather quizzically, looking up and then quickly back down.

"What's your father's name?" I queried further.

"Richard," she said with some surprise registering in her slightly longer gaze.

"What's your grandfather's name, on your father's side," I pursued, rather enjoying her growing curiosity.

"Benjamin," she offered, a tentative smile now on her mouth and a bit of wonder in her eyes.

"Benny Bragdon," I said, now eliciting a look of how do you… "Your grandfather was my father's best man at his and my mom's wedding in 1952."

That was my first new connection to this year's Honor's English IV class: just one person connecting with another person. Let me suggest this: we are good, not just here at Somersworth but at a lot of—maybe even most—schools, we are good at teaching quadratic equations, the Third Reich, the American Revolution, photosynthesis, algebra and geometry, anatomy, reading, writing, word processing, researching, MLA documentation, welding, landscaping, carpentry, yes, even sex education… all kinds of things to use in the proverbial "real world." I'm not sure we're always so good at teaching what it's really all about.

So what is it that it's really all about? Is this gathering, this ceremony, a celebration to commemorate your scholastic efforts of the last four years? Is it a sort of slap on the back to congratulate you for making it through? Or is it more like a memorial, a time to remember what has happened and the changes that have taken place during those years? Shoot, that could be kind of fun. We could talk about freshman year when Darren and some of you other little boys threw food around your lunch table, or the football players who had to run the swamp. Or we could talk about some of you getting dumped for the first time. Or Adam chipping his tooth or Corey nearly choking Justin to death, or Danielle peeing her pants in her sister's car, or Tyler growing to recognize that real men do wear pink!

Yeah, that stuff would be fun but this ceremony, this commencement, is designed not to mark an ending and to look back, but to mark the beginning and to look forward. And my role, I think, is to in some small way help you on your embarkation into the larger society. Let me say this: I believe that those of us who are really doing our jobs as teachers teach a little bit about our academic discipline and a whole lot about how to live life. I teach English, and those of you who have had me know that I teach it with passion, and high standards, and lots of work, and long papers, and very few A's. But it's not about proper MLA formatting and documentation; it's not about clear, well defined thesis statements, or successfully integrating quotes instead of simply inserting them; it's not about parallel construction, or identifying parts of speech, or avoiding run-on sentences, or knowing the etymology of, say, *pantheism*, or your SAT scores or your class rank. It's about relationships and connections and love. It's about Justine whose only wish for a present was to have the sixty bucks left from her final December paycheck for a bus ticket to go see her father for Christmas. It's about Josh learning about forgiveness even when he's not quite ready to do it. It's about Amy writing in a letter to me, "I had never really liked Hack. I don't know why, I just didn't. After being in this class, sitting next to him for ninety days, I learned he is such a nice kid and he loves everyone." It's about Kaylee who was not proud to be an unwed pregnant teen, but made the plan to finish high school, marry the baby's father, and begin to make the best home she could for them and their child. It's about James and me standing in a Greenland cemetery crying and hugging Tristan as we helped him say good-by to his mom. It's about Heather, whose answer to the question, *What is one thing about your life you would change if you could?* was to have a better relationship with her brother. It's about a whole class cheering as Ryan made an impressive and valiant ten-foot leap for a trapeze bar while standing on a twelve-inch-square platform—thirty feet up in the air! You know what? This end-of-the-class letter says it a hundred times better than I can:

Dear Mr. MacKenzie,

This class has changed me in ways that no other experience has ever done. Each unit offered me insights I had never known or had just plain overlooked. To tell you the truth I went through each day without a care in the world. Then we read books like **Tuesdays with Morrie** *and* **Way of the Peaceful Warrior** *and my outlook on life was changed indelibly.*

Another thing I took out of this class was the ability to love: to love friends, family, and even teachers. Now I can say it without being embarrassed or ashamed. Love ya, mean it,

Austin D.

Folks—those of you who had me in class may recall me saying to you that if you earn an F in my class you will have failed the course and that will be sad. But if you leave my class not knowing that I love and value you, then I will have failed you—and that will be tragic! Yes, I want smooth paragraph transitions, and properly cited quotes. I want you to speak clearly and deliberately, and to make good eye contact with your audience without using a lot of ums and ahs, and to say *nuclear,* not *nuculer*, but those are not, in the final analysis, the most important aspects of education, because if you do all of those things and don't love people it doesn't really matter. Morrie Schwartz recalled it this way: "Love is the only rational act." Shane, one of my sophomores, thought about that for a few moments one day and then said to me, "You know, that's kind of true." I said, "Yeah, it kind of is." People and relationships: *that's* what it's all about.

Morrie Schwartz's mantra was "Love each other or perish." Inherent in that admonition was the necessity to *be forgiving*. We got talking in class one day about forgiving and what forgiveness means, and we concluded that we don't really forgive for the other person or persons—we should forgive for ourselves. Because otherwise we let these petty little things just eat away at us and tear down relationships. I told a little story that day I'd first told to last year's seniors. It went something like this:

> Back in the early nineties I took some former tenants to small claims court because they left one of my apartments owing my wife and me what at the time was a fair amount of money—money we needed. I had a legitimate claim, presented my case before judge Clyde Coolidge, and won. Of course when I happened to run into Clyde at Pearl's Bakery the next morning he mentioned that I probably didn't want to start spending the money just yet. He was so right. They didn't pay me and so I had to go back to court for an order for periodic payments. I would get one or two at twenty-five bucks a pop and then they'd stop and I'd have to go back to court again. And this went on and on. The file MacKenzie vs. so-and-so got thicker and I got very little

money, and the times between the trips to court got longer and longer as I got more and more tired of the process. But to this day every time I open that drawer of my file cabinet and see that file it eats at me that they are getting away with stealing from us.

Now the truth is I can go back into court any time I want. There is no statute of limitations since I already have the judgment. Heck, it would be a simple matter now to just move to attach their property since I know they've bought a house. So here's my question: what would you guys do if you were me?

Well, one student said that I should take them back to court since it wasn't doing them any favor to let them go on believing you can cheat people and get away with it. Another said I should just forget it and stop letting it get to me, since by my own admission our real need for the money had long since passed. Still another suggested that I go ahead and get the attachment, as I would not be forcing them out of their home but only guaranteeing payment when they went to sell. Finally I turned to Josh and said, "Josh, care to weigh in on this. I'd be interested to hear your ideas." Josh thought for a minute and said, "Why don't you take the file, put it in a big fruit basket and send it to them?"

That's what it's all about folks: people and relationships. Corey did his final presentation on his grandfather, discussing how he saw every unit of his English course as having in some way intersected with his immediate circumstances. I want to share just the lead of Corey's personal narrative. It is titled *A Second Chance*:

The other day after getting home from school, I noticed a letter on my kitchen table. I could only make out the name Larry Francoeur so immediately I picked it up expecting it to be about jersey money or some code of conduct about how hazing freshmen will get me kicked off the football team. Needless to say I wasn't too thrilled to see this letter. But as I unfolded it and began to read

> *I was shocked to see that the letter wasn't for me at all, but for my grandfather, Leo Paul Guilmette. I had no idea what to think. What could Larry Francoeur, our school's Athletic Director, possibly have to say to my grandfather? As I read on I was amazed to learn that my grandfather would soon be inducted into the Somersworth Sports Hall of Fame. Turns out he played basketball, started all four years of football, and was the star centerfielder of his baseball team, hitting well over .300! This all came as quite a surprise to me considering I never knew my grandfather played any sports in high school. But that is only one of the many things I have learned about him over the last couple of months.*

You see, in order to deal with some health issues, Corey's grandparents moved into his house last year. In his paper he wrote, "*Most kids . . . would think having their grandparents move in with them their senior year of high school would be a nightmare.*" And, "*To be honest I did at first myself.*" But near the end of his paper he wrote, "*I cannot begin to describe how thankful I am to get this second chance to be close with my grandfather. I will never forget these past few months and all the time we've spent together. From the times we've sat down and eaten lunch together to the times we've both grown angry about the Red Sox's inability to win a championship, I will always remember getting this second chance to share with him. Honestly, I feel closer now than I ever have with both my grandmother and my grandfather.*" People and relationships: That's what it's all about.

I've been given a second chance, too. Remember that file I was telling you about? I never followed any of those suggestions. But here is the file, which I removed from my file cabinet this morning. I plan to call Westwind Gardens to order a fruit basket and send it along with the file to my former tenants. I have forgiven them for doing us wrong, and I am forgiving me for dwelling on this for such a ridiculously long period of time.

I told you about my first trip around the room on the first day of class last fall. Let me tell you about the last trip around the room, when I usually tell each student about something I will take away from my experiences with them. I got to this one young man and I asked him if

I could say what I wanted to say? He replied, “Go for it.” I said, “You may recall that early in the semester one of my questions-of-the-day was ‘What is one thing about your life you would change if you could?’ You responded that you would have your dad not live so far away. Another day you were sitting at my desk and we were just chatting. Your dad came up in conversation and you got a bit teary saying that it was pretty hard for you to talk about him, so we changed the subject. I used to feel sorry for you. But spending this semester with you, talking to you, hearing you share your thoughts and feelings, reading your papers, joking with you, and even crying with you once or twice I don’t feel sorry for you anymore; I feel sorry for your dad. People and relationships.

Members of the Class of 2004, I am deeply and permanently in your debt for how much you have enriched my life. I do love you. I do mean it, and *that*, once again, *is* what it’s all about.

Afterword

While I was working on this book I had a conversation with a former student turned friend. He knows that in many ways I am a fairly conservative guy and that I have actually become even more conservative since my teaching career began in 1993, an interesting phenomenon given the liberal tilt in much of academia. Most notably I have become a rabid advocate for the rights of kids. I think some of what we do to kids in our culture ought to be downright criminal. For example,

> No kid ought to be abused—physically, sexually, verbally
> No kid ought to have parents in jail
> No kid ought to suffer from neglect
> No kid ought to have to live in *fear* of parents who are drunk or on drugs
> Every kid has a *right* to their mother *and* their father—actively present in their life

As we talked about those things I could not help but think about Adam. Adam, whose mother was not married to his father and who had at some points in her life had serious problems with alcohol. Adam, whose father did not work, had a drug problem, and engaged in criminal activities to support his habit. Adam, whose father ended up in jail and once out, made the conscious decision to sign off and walk out of his life, whose father never paid a dime of support, never taught him to ride a bike or bait a hook, never took him to a ball game and never went to one of his games, never went to a teacher conference, a birthday celebration, or even to his funeral.

To the best of my knowledge, I have never laid eyes on Adam's father. I know his first name is Joe but know little else about him beyond the snippets I learned as I was gathering information for this book. I don't know if his life has been happy, sad, or utterly miserable. I do know that the picture he sent Adam when Adam was fifteen or sixteen showed him and the family he *chose* to make and then be a part of. There was a time when I'd love to have taken some verbal shots at him. I would have relished the opportunity.

I do know Charlene, reasonably well. I know that while she wanted me to write this book, she was worried that it would portray her as a bad mom. If it did, I did not do my job. Charlene wasn't a "bad mom," she was an "imperfect mom," a mom who did the best she could and who at the very least allowed her own family support system to help support her children as well. She was a mom who fiercely loved her children and wanted the best for them. She was a mom who brought herself to my classroom and to Sr. Becerra's classroom for meetings that I suspect made her very uncomfortable—but it was what her son needed. She was a mom who, for all of her imperfections, made many personal and financial sacrifices for her children.

There are also some things I want to say to Adam's father. I hope Joe discovers this book and reads it so I can apologize to him and seek his forgiveness for my harsh judgment. I hope that by him reading through all of the stories about Adam, experiencing all of the pain, laughter, tears, smiles, beauty, agony, and love they reveal, I've been able to introduce him to his son. I hope that in some small way he can understand how much we all loved that son, and perhaps then come to love him as well.

Maybe in a perfect world Adam would not have been born, so I guess I'm pretty darn glad it's not a perfect world.

ADAM

ROUTHIER

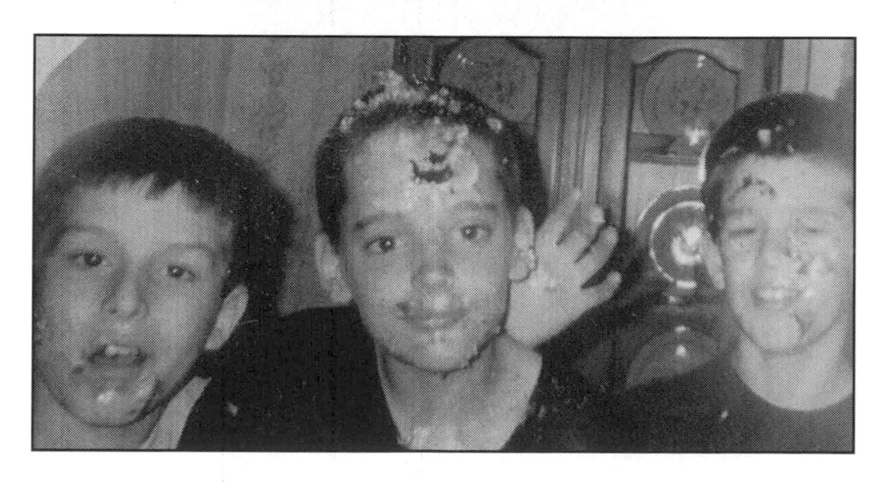

LITTLE LEAGUE

Congrats
GRAD

IN MEMORY OF

ADAM ROUTHIER

Made in the USA
Middletown, DE
27 June 2020

11218377R00099